THE WIZARD OF OZ

A Play in Three Acts

Dramatized by
ADELE THANE

From the Story by
L. FRANK BAUM

CAST OF CHARACTERS
(In Order of Speaking)

TOTO

DOROTHY

THREE MUNCHKINS

SCARECROW

WITCH OF THE NORTH

TIN WOODMAN

COWARDLY LION

SOLDIER WITH GREEN WHISKERS

WIZARD OF OZ

LADY

TWO WINKIES

WITCH OF THE WEST

MADAME WINKIE

GLINDA THE GOOD

AUNT EM

The premiere production of this play was given by the Boston Children's Theatre in 1952, under the direction of the author, Adele Thane. The play was then revised, and presented in its new form in 1956 by Seattle Junior Programs, under the direction of Mr. Kenneth Carr, of the University of Washington School of Drama.

The Wizard of Oz

PROLOGUE: Kansas.

(Toto rushes pell-mell through the house curtain, C., on all fours, barking. He is wearing a dunce cap. He bounds R. and barks, then crosses from R. to L., barking as he goes. Dorothy is heard calling offstage.)

DOROTHY *(off)*. Toto! Toto, come back here!

(She enters hastily through the curtain, C., carrying a geography book. She is dressed in a blue-and-white checked gingham playfrock, white apron and stockings, and old Mary-Janes. A handkerchief is in the pocket of her apron. She stamps her foot at Toto who is just disappearing through the exit L.)

Come back here this instant!

(Toto backs up slowly.)

Come on now.

(Toto continues to back up until he is just in front of Dorothy, then he sits on her foot, which is tapping an exasperated tattoo on the floor.)

The very idea! Running away from your geography lesson like that! Aren't you ashamed?

(Toto hangs his head and whimpers. Dorothy points to his dunce cap.)

Do you want to be a dunce all your life?

(Toto throws back his head and howls a statement.)

What's that? You don't care two ham bones about being an educated dog.

(Toto barks in the affirmative, then adds another comment.)

You just want to be Dorothy's dog. But that's just it, Toto—you are my dog, and I insist that you—be—educated. There!

(Dorothy lightly thumps Toto's nose for emphasis.)

Now then, where were we?

(She kneels down beside him and opens the geography book.)

Here we are. What state do we live in?

(Toto doesn't understand the question.)

Where do we live?

(Toto sneezes something that sounds like "Oz-z-z-z!")

In the land of Oz?

(Toto barks "Yes!")

Who ever heard of such a place. No—We live in Kansas.

(Toto repeats "Kansas" in his dog language.)

Can you tell me where Kansas is?

(Toto barks a reply that sets Dorothy back on her heels in disgust.)

In New Zealand! Toto, really!

(Getting to her feet.)

It's in the United States, a long way west of Boston. It's prairie land—gray, and sun-baked, and flat. Very, very flat.

(She closes the geography book and holds it out level.)

In fact, if it were a pancake, you could pour syrup on it, and the syrup would never run off!—that's how flat it is.

(Toto laps the surface of the book noisily as if it were covered with syrup.)

And right in the middle of the flattest part, live Aunt Em and Uncle Henry. And me. And you.

(Toto whines in delight.)

And do you know what else there is in Kansas?

(Toto shakes his head.)

Cyclones!

(Toto gives four sharp barks.)

What's a cyclone? Well—

(Dorothy turns R. and looks out front.)

Imagine that you can hear a low wail of the wind in the north, and can see the long grass bending in waves to the ground.

(Wind: fade in low on front speakers. Dorothy turns L.)

Now, there comes a sharp whistling in the air from the south, and the grass ripples in that direction, too.

(Wind: slight crescendo. Dorothy cocks her head and listens. Toto barks.)

Shhhhh! Listen, Toto! Isn't that the wind?

(Wind: crescendo. Suddenly Dorothy points out front.)

Look, Toto, look! It's a cyclone coming! We've got to get home. Come on! Hurry!

(They dash off R.)

Wind: increases in volume to a shriek.

Thunder.

Lights dim to blackout.

House Curtain opens.

The full stage is seen in a faint light, with only the front steps and porch of Dorothy's house clearly defined DL.

Lightning. Thunder.

Wind: mounts in intensity. The branch of a tree crashes to the ground.

(Toto tears across the stage from UR. to DL., barking frantically. Another branch falls to the ground, just missing him, and he cowers in a corner by the porch steps, whimpering with terror, his head between his paws. Dorothy is heard calling off UR.)

Toto! Toto! Wait for me! Wait!

(She runs on.)

Where are you?

(Toto crawls toward her. Wind: crescendo.)

Toto! You'll be blown away!

(Dorothy herself is being buffeted about by the wind.)

Quick! Quick! Run for the cellar!

(Dorothy and Toto struggle over to the porch steps. Lightning. Thunder.)

Aunt Em! Uncle Henry!

(Dorothy and Toto start swaying from side to side on the porch.)

Ooooh, the house is shaking! It's whirling around!

(Dorothy clutches Toto by the collar and hangs on for dear life.)

Hold on, Toto! Hold on! We're going up!—up—UP!

(Dorothy rises on her tiptoes, lifting her arms over her head. Toto howls.)

Aunty Em! AUNT-EEEE EM!

(Lightning. Thunder. Blackout. Wind: reaches a peak, then slowly subsides as Lights come up on ACT ONE: Scene 1.)

7

ACT ONE

SCENE 1.

Land of the Munchkins. Morning. Bright sunshine. Blue sky.

*Front of Dorothy's house (door and porch), DL. Tree and bench,
R. A field fence, painted blue, runs across the back, with opening
C. Ground row. Wood wings UL. and UR.*

*A pair of silver slippers are sticking out from under the porch
steps of the house.*

*Lights come up on an empty stage. Then UR., behind the fence,
three Munchkin men enter, cautiously. They are dressed in
blue, and wear blue round hats that rise to a small point a
foot above their heads, with little bells around the brims that
tinkle as they move. On their feet are well-polished black boots,
with a deep roll of blue at the tops. Two of the men have beards,
the third is smooth-shaven.*

*They pause C., in the opening of the fence, and whisper together,
looking apprehensively toward the house. The smooth-shaven
Munchkin takes the lead, and approaches the porch. He puts out
a timid finger and pokes one of the silver slippers. Growing bolder
he pokes the other. Now fully reassured, he pinches the toe of
each slipper, and turns to his companions, who have been standing
at a safe distance, C.*

FIRST MUNCHKIN *(in an excited whisper)*. She's dead. The Witch
of the East is dead!

(Munchkins cheer and go into a spirited dance.)

MUNCHKINS *(chanting)*.
Blueberry muffins and caraway bread,
The Witch of the East is dead, dead, dead;
Click your heels and duck your head,
The Witch of the East is dead, dead, dead;
I said, you said, we three together said:
The Witch of the East is dead, dead, dead!

*(While the Munchkins are dancing, Dorothy opens the door of
the house, curiously, and she and Toto peep out. Dorothy is fas-
cinated by the little men; she tiptoes across the porch to the steps,
followed by Toto.*

*The Munchkins become aware of Dorothy's presence, and stop
dancing. They line up, remove their hats, place one hand over
the heart, and bow ceremoniously.*

Dorothy curtsies, not knowing what else to do.

*At that moment, a little old woman, the Witch of the North, enters
UR. above the fence, trots, rather than walks, to the C. opening*

8

and stops. She is dressed all in white, and wears a white hat similar in style to the Munchkins' hats; her gown is sprinkled with little stars that glisten like diamonds. She is carrying a long wand, like a staff, with a large letter "N" on the tip.

The Munchkins, as one man, turn upstage and bow to her. She trots over to the foot of the porch steps, smiles up at Dorothy, and bows low. Munchkins bow, too, and put on their hats.)

WITCH OF THE NORTH. Welcome, noble Sorceress, to the Land of the Munchkins.

DOROTHY *(skipping down the porch steps, laughing).* Oh, I'm not a sorceress. I'm Dorothy.

(Toto sits on the top step of the porch, interested in everything that goes on around him).

WITCH OF THE NORTH. We are grateful to you for killing the wicked Witch of the East. You have set us free.

DOROTHY *(with wonder).* Did I kill—a witch?

WITCH OF THE NORTH *(laughing).* Your house did, and that's the same thing.

(She points to the porch steps).

See! There are her two feet sticking out in their silver slippers.

DOROTHY *(dismayed).* Oh, dear! The house must have fallen on her. What shall we do?

WITCH OF THE NORTH *(calmly, leading Dorothy away C.).* Do? Nothing, my dear. Nothing at all.

DOROTHY. But who was she?

WITCH OF THE NORTH. I've told you. She was the wicked Witch of the East.

(Indicating Munchkins) For years, she ruled over the Munchkins, and made them her slaves. Now they are all set free.

DOROTHY *(looking inquiringly at the Munchkins).* Who are the Munchkins?

WITCH OF THE NORTH. They are the people who live in this land of the East.

DOROTHY. Are you a Munchkin?

WITCH OF THE NORTH *(smiling warmly at the Munchkins, laying her hand on First Munchkin's shoulder).* No—but I'm their friend.

DOROTHY *(anxiously).* Are you a—a witch?

WITCH OF THE NORTH *(gaily).* Yes, indeed! I'm the Witch of the North.

(Reassuringly, as Dorothy recoils) But I'm a good witch, and the people love me.

DOROTHY *(still frightened)*. But I thought all witches were wicked.

(Witch of the North goes to Dorothy and leads her gently over to the bench under the tree, explaining patiently. Munchkins line up behind the bench).

WITCH OF THE NORTH. Oh, no! The Witch of the South is good, too. You see—

(Witch of the North and Dorothy sit).

—there were four witches in the Land of Oz—Two good ones, and two bad ones. Your house has killed one of the bad ones. So now there's only one wicked witch left—the Witch of the West.

DOROTHY *(politely, but firmly)*. But Aunt Em says there aren't any witches nowadays.

WITCH OF THE NORTH *(shortly)*. Who is Aunt Em?

DOROTHY. She lives in Kansas, and I live with her.

(Sadly, looking at the house) Or I did.

WITCH OF THE NORTH. Kansas?

(She thinks for a moment).

I've never heard of that country before. Is it civilized?

DOROTHY. Oh, yes.

WITCH OF THE NORTH. Then that accounts for it! I've heard there are no witches left in civilized countries. But, you see, the Land of Oz has never been civilized. So it still has witches and wizards.

DOROTHY. Wizards, too?

WITCH OF THE NORTH *(nodding, her voice sinking to a whisper)*. Yes! Oz himself is the Great Wizard. He lives in the Emerald City.

DOROTHY. Is the Emerald City—

(Suddenly the Munchkins, who have been standing silently by, give a shout, and point to the silver slippers. Toto pricks up his ears, rears up on his hind legs, and looks over the porch railing).

WITCH OF THE NORTH *(rising)*. What is it?

(She crosses L. to the porch, looks down, and begins to laugh. Dorothy has risen, and stands uncertainly downstage of the bench.

Toto scampers down the porch steps and snuffles the ground around the silver slippers).

(beckoning to Dorothy, still laughing) Come here, my dear.

10

(Dorothy crosses L., and stands beside the Witch, looking down at the spot the witch is pointing to.

Toto barks and rushes out of the corner, sits on his haunches in front of Dorothy, holding up the silver slippers in his mouth).

DOROTHY *(amazed)*. Why—why, the feet of the Witch have disappeared, and nothing is left but her slippers!

WITCH OF THE NORTH. She was so old, she dried up like water in the sun. Well, that's the end of her! But the silver slippers are yours, my dear, and you shall have them to wear.

(She reaches down and takes the slippers from Toto. After shaking the dust out of them, she hands them to Dorothy).

The Witch of the East was proud of these slippers. I think they have a magic charm, but I don't know what it is.

DOROTHY *(examining the slippers)*. I wonder if they'll fit.

WITCH OF THE NORTH. Why don't you try them on?

DOROTHY. I will.

(She crosses to the bench and sits. First Munchkin kneels in front of her and removes her old shoes, giving them to Second Munchkin. As First Munchkin is fitting one of the silver slippers on Dorothy's foot, Toto bounds over and snatches the other one in his mouth, then proceeds to run around the stage, pursued by the Munchkins).

(rising and stamping her foot) Toto! You naughty dog! Bring back that slipper! Bring it here to me!

(Toto disregards the command and continues to elude the Munchkins, but finally they corner him and tug at the slipper which is clamped between his teeth with bulldog tenacity).

(to Toto) Let go of it, Toto! Let go of it, I say!

(Toto suddenly releases the slipper and the Munchkins fall over backward).

Shame on you, Toto! Sha-a-a-a-me!

(Toto whimpers and drops his head between his paws).

Now go over and sit on that porch with your nose to the door, and don't you dare turn around or even quiver a whisker this way—not a whisker. Do you hear?

(Toto meekly crawls over to the porch and sits with hanging head, facing the door.

The Munchkins pick themselves up and return to the bench, where Dorothy reseats herself to have the second slipper fitted on by the First Munchkin. When this is done, he goes and stands beside the other Munchkins. Dorothy stretches out her legs before her, admiring the slippers).

11

WITCH OF THE NORTH. They fit perfectly, my dear.

(Dorothy stands and walks downstage, flexing her toes).

DOROTHY. They're just the thing for a long walk.

WITCH OF THE NORTH. Where are you walking to?

DOROTHY. Well, I want to get back to my aunt and uncle. I'm sure they're worried about me. Can you help me find the way?

(Munchkins and Witch first look at one another, and then at Dorothy. They shake their heads).

FIRST MUNCHKIN *(turning and pointing DL.).* To the East, lies a great desert.

SECOND MUNCHKIN *(turning and pointing DR.).* To the South, the woods are full of wild beasts.

THIRD MUNCHKIN *(turning and pointing UR.).* To the West, the country is ruled by the Wicked Witch. She would make you her slave if you passed that way.

(Dorothy turns to Witch of the North).

DOROTHY. And—the North?

WITCH OF THE NORTH. It's the same. The great desert is all around this Land of Oz.

(She moves to Dorothy and pats her shoulder).

I'm afraid, my dear, that you'll have to live with us.

DOROTHY *(choking up).* Thank you—you're very kind, but—

(she bursts out crying)

—I want to go home.

(Dorothy puts her fists in her eyes, sobbing. Her tears seem to grieve the Munchkins, for they immediately take out handkerchiefs and begin to weep also, each dropping his head on the other's shoulder. Witch of the North stands perplexed for a moment, then takes off her hat and balances the point of it on the tip of her nose).

WITCH OF THE NORTH *(counting in a solemn voice).* One. Two. Three.

(She stands tense, as if listening. The wailing of Dorothy and the Munchkins annoys her. She raises her hand irritably).

Shhhhhh!

(Dorothy and the Munchkins quiet down. There is dead silence. Then a Voice speaks out of nowhere).

VOICE. Let Dorothy go to the Emerald City.

WITCH OF THE NORTH. Ah!

(She claps her hat back on her head).

There! Now you know where to go. Perhaps Oz will help you.

(Dorothy snuffles, trying to smile. The Munchkins surround her and dry her eyes with their handkerchiefs).

FIRST MUNCHKIN *(his handkerchief to her nose).* Blow!

(Dorothy does so, and the Munchkins blow their noses, too. Then they retire to their former positions locking arms and crossing the left foot over the right).

DOROTHY *(to Witch).* Where is the Emerald City?

WITCH OF THE NORTH *(pointing DL. with her wand).* It's exactly in the center of the country, and is ruled by Oz, the Great Wizard.

DOROTHY *(anxiously).* Is he a good man?

WITCH OF THE NORTH. He's a good Wizard. Whether he's a man or not, I can't say, for I've never seen him.

DOROTHY. How can I get there?

WITCH OF THE NORTH. You must walk.

(She smiles down at the silver slippers on Dorothy's feet. Dorothy stoops and polishes the slippers with the hem of her dress).

DOROTHY *(confidently).* Oh, my silver slippers will take me there, all right.

WITCH OF THE NORTH. It's a long, long journey, and sometimes it will be dark and terrible.

(Dorothy straightens up, disturbed. The Witch puts an arm around her reassuringly).

But your silver slippers will get you there.

(Points off DL.) Just follow the yellow brick road.

DOROTHY. I'd better take something to eat. Excuse me a minute.

(She runs L. into the house. The Witch listens to the Munchkins talking together).

SECOND MUNCHKIN. She must be a great Sorceress.

THIRD MUNCHKIN *(nodding).* Yes. She has white in her dress, the good-witch color.

FIRST MUNCHKIN. And blue—the Munchkin color.

SECOND MUNCHKIN *(crossing to the Witch).* Witch of the North, shouldn't we go with her?

WITCH OF THE NORTH. It's better to keep away from Oz, unless you have business with him.

13

SECOND MUNCHKIN. But the danger—

WITCH OF THE NORTH *(calmly)*. My magic will protect her.

THIRD MUNCHKIN *(crossing to Second Munchkin)*. Couldn't we go just part of the way?

WITCH OF THE NORTH. Who would harvest your corn?

(Dorothy enters from the house, carrying a little basket of bread and cheese, covered with a white napkin. A pink sunbonnet is over her arm. She crosses to the Witch).

DOROTHY. There! I guess I'm all ready.

(She starts DL., hesitates, and turns back to the Witch pleadingly).

Won't you come with me?

WITCH OF THE NORTH *(shaking her head)*. I can't.

(She goes to Dorothy).

But I'll give you my kiss, and no one will dare to hurt you.

(She kisses Dorothy gently on the forehead).

Goodbye, my dear. Remember—take the yellow brick road. When you get to Oz, don't be afraid of him. Tell him your story, and ask him to help you.

(Dorothy looks past the Witch to the Munchkins, and curtsies).

DOROTHY. Goodbye, little Munchkin men.

MUNCHKINS *(bowing low, hats in hand)*. Goodbye. Have a pleasant journey.

DOROTHY *(to Witch)*. Dear good Witch. Thank you for everything.

(The Witch gives Dorothy a friendly little nod, and waves her DL. with her wand. The Munchkins raise their hats high. Dorothy whistles to Toto, who has been sitting on the porch steps, and he bounds to her side, barking).

The House Curtain closes.

Dorothy is L. on the apron. She looks down the aisle, sets down her basket, and ties on her sunbonnet).

Well, come along, Toto. We'll go to the Emerald City and ask the great Oz how to get back to Kansas.

(She is starting down the steps when the First Munchkin pokes his head through the C. opening of the curtain).

FIRST MUNCHKIN. Pssssst! Dorothy! Wait for me.

(He crosses to her).

14

The yellow brick road runs right by my farm. We'll go along together.

DOROTHY. Oh, that will be fun!

FIRST MUNCHKIN. Let me carry your basket.

(She gives it to him).

Come on.

(They start down the aisle, with Toto barking and running on ahead. They exit through the rear door.

The House Curtain opens. Behind it, the Act Curtain is closed).

ACT ONE

SCENE 2.

A Cornfield. Afternoon.

The Scarecrow is in position in front of the Act Curtain. An old pointed blue hat is perched on his head. He is dressed in a blue Munchkin suit, faded and worn, and on his feet are some old boots with blue tops; on his hands, white gloves. He is held upright by means of a pole thrust vertically down his back, and a crosspiece stuck through the sleeves of his coat.

After a moment, he heaves a sigh, turns his head L., and winks at the audience with one eye; then turns his head R., and winks with the other eye. He calls out.

SCARECROW. Yoo-hoo!

(He waves his hands up and down from the wrists, and does a little dance step in place. Suddenly he stops his antics, looks toward the rear of the Stage Right aisle, and exclaims).

Oh-oh!

(Assuming his former limp pose, he stands perfectly still. The rear door, Stage Right aisle opens, and Dorothy, and the First Munchkin enter. Dorothy's sunbonnet is pushed off her head and hangs down her back by the streamers).

FIRST MUNCHKIN *(walking into view).* You'll be able to see my farm from the top of this hill.

(He stops and points to the stage).

There! That's it—over to the left.

DOROTHY. My goodness, it's beautiful!

FIRST MUNCHKIN *(proudly, leading the way down the aisle).* It's the biggest farm in Munchkin land.

(Outside the auditorium door, behind them, a sharp barking is heard).

DOROTHY. Toto! Toto, what is it?

(Several quick barks).

He's found something. Look, he's digging!

FIRST MUNCHKIN. Oh, that's all right. That's where I used to keep my bone meal. I need a hole dug there, anyway. Keep digging, boy!

DOROTHY. Hurry up, Toto. When you've finished, you must catch up with me.

(Toto answers, and Dorothy and the First Munchkin proceed down the aisle, toward the stage).

FIRST MUNCHKIN. We are coming to my corn field.

DOROTHY. But it's blue!

FIRST MUNCHKIN. Of course. What colour would it be? Every thing in Munchkin Land is blue.

DOROTHY. Oh!

(They reach the SR. steps, First Munchkin walks to C., and indicates the Scarecrow).

FIRST MUNCHKIN. I put him up yesterday. What do you think of him?

DOROTHY *(crosses to peer at Scarecrow).* He looks all right to me.

(As she speaks, she turns to Munchkin, so that her back is to the Scarecrow; Munchkin is looking at Dorothy, so that neither one of them sees the Scarecrow's reaction, which is to cock his head on one side and grin at the audience).

FIRST MUNCHKIN. How do you like his ears?

DOROTHY *(examining them).* They aren't straight—

(turns back to Munchkin apologetically) are they?

(Appropriate reaction from Scarecrow, unseen by Dorothy and Munchkin).

FIRST MUNCHKIN. Never mind. They're ears just the same.

DOROTHY *(anxious to say something complimentary, scrutinizes Scarecrow carefully).* His eyes are rather pretty.

(turns to Munchkin enthusiastically) Blue paint is just the color for eyes.

(Appropriate reaction from Scarecrow).

16

FIRST MUNCHKIN (*confidentially, lowering his voice—Scarecrow cocks his ear to listen*). I made one eye a leetle bigger than the other.

(*Scarecrow reacts*).

He'll scare the crows away fast enough.

(*Looking at Scarecrow*).

He looks just like a man.

DOROTHY (*Smiles at Scarecrow, then at Munchkin*). Why, he is a man!

(*Big reaction from Scarecrow*).

FIRST MUNCHKIN (*giving Dorothy her basket*). Well, I must be seeing to the stock. You're sure you won't stop in and meet the missus?

DOROTHY (*shaking her head*). No, I'm sorry. I must be on my way, if I ever want to get back to Kansas.

FIRST MUNCHKIN (*dubiously*). I hope you do. Well—

(*shaking hands*) goodbye, Dorothy, my dear. Good luck!

DOROTHY. Goodbye, Mr. Boq.

(*First Munchkin exits R. Dorothy looks after him, then at the Scarecrow, sighs, and starts to cross L.*).

SCARECROW (*in a husky voice*). Hullo, Dorothy!

(*Dorothy stops in surprise. She looks up and down and around, trying to locate where the voice came from. The Scarecrow nods to her in a friendly way. She approaches him in wonder*).

DOROTHY. Did—did you speak?

SCARECROW (*waving his hand*). Certainly. How do you know?

DOROTHY (*politely, but breathlessly*). I'm pretty well, thank you. How do you do?

SCARECROW. Not well at all. I'm tired of being up here.

DOROTHY. Can't you get down?

SCARECROW. No. There's a pole stuck down my back—and another across my shoulders. Will you please take them away?

(*Dorothy reaches up and pulls out the pole stuck through his sleeves first, then together they remove the pole from his back. Dorothy sets down the poles, and the Scarecrow promptly collapses in a heap, laughing merrily. Dorothy picks him up, setting him on his feet again*).

17

Thank you, thank you very much.

(He stretches and yawns).

I feel like a new man. If I had any brains, I'd have thought of a way to get down myself.

DOROTHY *(surprised)*. Haven't you any brains?

SCARECROW *(sadly)*. No. You see, I'm stuffed, so I have no brains at all.

DOROTHY *(sympathetically)*. Oh, I'm awfully sorry. ˇ

SCARECROW *(perking up)*. Where are you going?

DOROTHY. To the Emerald City, to ask Oz to send me back to Kansas.

SCARECROW *(bending down to Dorothy eagerly)*. Do you think— if I go to the Emerald City with you—that Oz would give me some brains?

DOROTHY. I don't know—

(generously) but you may come with me, if you like. Even if Oz doesn't give you any brains, you'll be no worse off than you are now.

SCARECROW. That's true.

(confidently) You see, I don't mind my legs and arms and body being stuffed, because I can't get hurt. If anyone steps on my toes or sticks a pin in me, it doesn't matter—I can't feel it.

(He crosses to RC. earnestly).

But I don't want to be a fool, and if my head stays stuffed with straw, how am I ever going to know anything?

DOROTHY *(crossing to Scarecrow, truly sorry for him)*. Well, then, you just come along with me, and I'll ask Oz to do all he can to help you.

SCARECROW *(gratefully)*. Thank you.

(Dorothy sits on the R. stage steps and unpacks her basket of bread and cheese).

DOROTHY. Let's eat before we start. I'm hungry. Aren't you?

SCARECROW *(shaking his head)*. No, I'm never hungry. And a lucky thing, too—because if I should cut a hole in my mouth so I could eat, the straw would come out, and that would spoil the shape of my head.

(He laughs good-naturedly, and Dorothy joins in, eating all the while. Scarecrow sits on the apron of the stage, L. of Dorothy).

Tell me something about this Kansas country you come from.

DOROTHY *(swallowing a piece of bread)*. Well, it's prairie land, and—

SCARECROW *(interrupting)*. What's prairie?

DOROTHY. Open country—like around here—only there aren't any trees, or hills, or pretty flowers. The sun burns everything to a dull gray. Even the grass isn't green.

SCARECROW *(clucking disapprovingly)*. Tch, tch, tch!

DOROTHY. There are dreadful wind storms, called cyclones, that can blow a house right up into the sky and carry it away. That's how I got here.

SCARECROW *(scratching his head)*. Golly! I can't understand why you want to leave this beautiful place and go back there.

DOROTHY *(gently)*. If you had brains, you'd understand. It doesn't matter to me how dreary my home is. I'd rather live there than anywhere else in the world. There's no place like home.

(She sighs and starts packing up her basket, keeping out a piece of bread for Toto. She calls for him).

Toto! Here, Toto! It's time to go. Here, Toto, I've got something for you.

(she holds out the bread for Toto. The Scarecrow takes it).

SCARECROW. Thanks. Though my name isn't Toto, you know.

(Cheerfully) It's lucky for me that you did live in Kansas, or the cyclone wouldn't have blown you here to pull me off my stake.

DOROTHY. Well, let's go, shall we?

SCARECROW. Do let me carry that basket. It's no trouble, because I can't get tired.

(He takes the basket from Dorothy. Toto comes bounding in, down the aisle, and springs up on the stage, barking eagerly. He quite startles the Scarecrow, who has never seen a dog before. He cries out and points).

DOROTHY. Don't mind Toto. He never bites.

SCARECROW. I couldn't feel it if he did.

(He laughs uproariously and bends down to Dorothy, close to her ear).

I'll tell you a secret. There's only one thing in the world I'm afraid of.

DOROTHY. What's that?

19

SCARECROW *(looking over his shoulder to make sure they are alone, whispering).* A lighted match!

(He turns to go upstage C., and bumps into the Act Curtain. He loses his balance and falls flat).

Oooooops!

(Dorothy runs to pick him up, followed by Toto).

I didn't see that.

(On his hands and knees, he looks down at the stage directly in front of the C. opening in the curtain).

The road goes through here.

(He gets to his feet, with the help of Dorothy, and begins pawing the curtain, trying to find the C. opening).

If it comes out, it must go in.

DOROTHY. Anyone would know that.

SCARECROW. Certainly. That's why I know it. If I needed brains to figure it out, I'd never have said it.

(He puts his shoulder against the curtain, pushing in pantomime, and grunting. Dorothy gets behind him and pushes, too. Toto gets behind Dorothy and pushes. The Act Curtain opens, and Scarecrow, Dorothy and Toto fall into—)

ACT ONE

Scene 3.

Edge of the Forest. Afternoon.

Tree UR., as in Scene 1. Blue fence has been swung down C., and now runs at an angle from UC. down to LC., and off L. Tree stump down LC., below fence. Log C., Rocks DR. Sky is still blue. Wood wings up back, L. and R. Ground row.

The Tin Woodman is standing slightly behind and L. of the tree, with an uplifted axe in his hands. He stands perfectly motionless. Dorothy and Scarecrow disentangle themselves. This time Scarecrow helps Dorothy to her feet. She is rubbing her shins.

Toto limps to stump LC. and sits.

SCARECROW *(to Dorothy).* Oh, dear! Did you hurt yourself?

DOROTHY. Just a little.

(Tin Woodman groans. Dorothy stops nursing her shins, and looks at Scarecrow anxiously).

Are you hurt, too?

20

SCARECROW. Oh, no! Nothing can hurt straw.

(Woodman groans again).

DOROTHY. Then why are you groaning?

SCARECROW. I'm not groaning. That was you.

DOROTHY. No, it wasn't. Listen!

(Woodman gives a really piercing groan. Dorothy turns UR).

It came from over there.

(She starts up to the tree, followed by Scarecrow. They see Tin Woodman, and stop short, with cries of surprise).

(to Woodman). Did you groan?

WOODMAN *(in a squeaky voice).* Yes, I did. I've been groaning for over a year now, and no one has ever heard me before.

DOROTHY. You poor thing! What can we do?

WOODMAN. Get an oil can and oil my joints.

DOROTHY *(blankly).* An oil can?

WOODMAN *(impatiently).* Yes, yes! My joints are rusted.

DOROTHY *(looking around helplessly).* Where is it?

WOODMAN. Somewhere!

(In desperation).

Find it! Find it!

(Scarecrow sets down the basket and he and Dorothy run about the stage, hunting for the oil can. Toto joins in, sniffling along the L. length of the fence. Dorothy searches among the rocks DR.; Scarecrow rummages around the log C. Then Dorothy runs over to the tree stump to continue her search, while Scarecrow gallops UC. around the fence and behind it, stumbling and sprawling. Toto follows him, sniffing from L. to R., and UC.).

(spurring them on) Hurry! Hurry! My joints are rusted so badly, I can't move! If I'm oiled, I'll be all right.

(Toto discovers the oil can behind the fence and barks excitedly).

SCARECROW. Here it is! Toto found it!

(He hurries with it toward Woodman, followed by Toto. He trips over Toto and falls. Dorothy rescues the oil can).

DOROTHY *(to Woodman).* Where shall I begin?

WOODMAN. Oil my neck first.

(Dorothy oils Woodman's neck. Scarecrow takes hold of the tin

21

head and moves it gently from side to side until it works freely. Sound: Squeak of rusty metal).

WOODMAN. Now oil my arms.

(Dorothy oils Woodman's elbows, and Scarecrow bends them carefully. Sound: Squeak of rusty metal).

(giving a sigh of satisfaction and lowering his axe) I've been holding that axe in the air ever since I rusted. I'm sure glad to put it down at last.

(Scarecrow relieves him of the axe).

Now, if you'll oil my legs—

(Dorothy oils Woodman's knees and ankles, and he limbers up, to the accompaniment of squeaks. Sound: creaking metal joints).

(The Woodman tries out his legs, walking stiffly to the log. Dorothy and Scarecrow hover near to support him in case he should falter).

Thank you. Thank you. I might have stood here forever if you hadn't come along.

DOROTHY. Don't you want your jaws oiled? Your voice squeaks dreadfully—like chalk on a blackboard.

(Scarecrow shudders).

WOODMAN *(eagerly).* Yes, yes, of course!

(Dorothy oils his jaws, and the Woodman practices the vocalists' "mi-mi-mi" exercise until his voice comes clear and natural).

Ah! that's better! You've saved my life. How'd you happen to be here?

DOROTHY. We're on our way to the Emerald City, to see the Wizard of Oz.

WOODMAN. What for?

DOROTHY. I want him to send me back to Kansas—

SCARECROW *(breaking in).* And I want him to put a few brains in my head.

(Woodman crosses slowly to the tree stump, thinking deeply. He sits. Dorothy and Scarecrow exchange puzzled glances. Dorothy sets down the oil can beside the log).

WOODMAN *(finally).* Do you suppose Oz could give me a heart?

DOROTHY *(crossing to him).* Why, I guess so. It would be as easy as to give the Scarecrow brains.

(Scarecrow agrees heartily, going over to stand beside Dorothy).

WOODMAN *(to Scarecrow, shaking his head dolefully).* Brains aren't the best things in the world.

SCARECROW *(crossing behind Woodman and feeling his head)*. Do you have any?

WOODMAN. No, my head's quite empty. But once I had brains—and a heart, too. *(Sighs)* I'd much rather have a heart.

SCARECROW. Why?

WOODMAN. I'll tell you my story. Once I was a real man—and I loved a Munchkin girl. But the wicked Witch of the East didn't want us to marry. So she laid an evil spell on my axe.

(He takes the axe from the Scarecrow).

DOROTHY. That axe?

WOODMAN *(nodding)*. Yes. First it cut off my leg. I had to find a tinsmith who could make me a new one. Then it cut off my other leg, and I called in the tinsmith again. Next, the axe cut off my arms, and then my head, and so it went. But alas, the tinsmith couldn't make me a heart, and I lost my love for the Munchkin girl.

DOROTHY *(warmly, touched by his story)*. I'm sure Oz can help you. Come with us.

(She helps him to his feet).

SCARECROW *(starting UC.)*. All the same, I shall ask for brains instead of a heart. A fool wouldn't know what to do with a heart if he had one.

(He crosses to the tree and picks up the basket, then comes down R. of the log).

WOODMAN *(starting C., arm in arm with Dorothy)*. I'll take the heart.

(All three start UC. but are arrested by a sharp bark from Toto at the log).

DOROTHY. What is it, Toto?

(Toto barks again, pointing behind the log with his paw).

WOODMAN. My oil can!

DOROTHY. Shall you be needing it any more?

WOODMAN. Better take it along. I don't want to rust again, and it's likely to rain. That's what happened last time.

(Scarecrow puts the oil can in the basket, and all three start UC. toward the Exit UL., followed proudly by Toto. Scarecrow, leading the way, stumbles into a hole and rolls over. Dorothy and Woodman help him up).

WOODMAN. Why didn't you walk around the hole?

SCARECROW *(cheerfully)*. I don't know enough. My head is stuffed with straw.

(He starts off UL. suddenly there is a terrible roar off UL., and the Cowardly Lion bounds onstage. With one blow of his paw, he knocks over Scarecrow. Then he strikes Woodman, who falls down and lies still. Toto runs barking toward the Lion, who bares his teeth to bite him. Dorothy rushes forward and slaps the Lion on his nose).

DOROTHY *(with spirit).* Don't you dare bite Toto! You ought to be ashamed of yourself! A big beast like you, biting a poor little dog!

LION *(rubbing his nose).* I didn't bite him!

DOROTHY. No, but you tried to. You're nothing but a big coward!

LION *(hanging his head).* I know it.

DOROTHY *(scolding).* And to think of your striking a straw man!

(Dorothy goes over to assist Scarecrow, who is struggling to his feet. She walks him down to R. of the Lion).

LION *(surprised).* Is he straw?

DOROTHY *(putting Scarecrow into shape).* Of course he's straw.

LION. So that's why he went over so easily. Is the other one stuffed, too?

(Dorothy runs over to Woodman, and steadies him into position L. of Lion).

DOROTHY. No, he's made of tin.

LION. Tin! *(He sucks his claws).* He nearly blunted my claws. It made the cold shivers run down my spine. Brrrrr!

SCARECROW *(shuddering, too).* Brrrrr!

LION *(indicating Toto).* And is that thing made of tin—or stuffed?

DOROTHY *(tartly).* Neither. He's a real dog.

(Lion straddles the log, and drops into a crouching position, sniffling and wiping his nose with the tip of his tail).

LION. Oh, I am a coward, or I wouldn't have tried to bite a real little dog!

DOROTHY *(gazing at Lion in wonder).* What makes you a coward?

LION. I don't know. *(he wipes his eyes with his tail)* A Lion is supposed to be the King of Beasts. But I'm scared of everything!

SCARECROW. That isn't right, you know. The King of the Beasts should have courage.

LION *(tearfully).* I know it. But whenever I meet an elephant, or a tiger, or—or a man, my heart begins to beat like anything.

WOODMAN. Perhaps you have heart disease.

24

LION *(blubbering)*. P-P-Perhaps.

WOODMAN. If you have, you ought to be glad, because it proves you have a heart. I haven't.

(He heaves a great sigh).

LION *(thoughtfully, looking up)*. Maybe—if I didn't have a heart, I wouldn't be a coward.

SCARECROW *(eagerly)*. Have you any brains?

LION *(feeling his head)*. I suppose so. I've never looked to see.

SCARECROW. I'm going to the great Oz, to ask him to give me some.

WOODMAN. And I'm going, to ask him for a heart.

DOROTHY. And I'm going, to ask him to send me back to Kansas.

LION *(rising, hopefully)*. Do you think Oz would give me—courage?

SCARECROW. Just as easily as he could give me brains.

WOODMAN. Or me, a heart.

DOROTHY. Or send me back to Kansas.

LION *(stepping clear of the log)*. Then, if you don't mind, I'll go along with you. *(whimpering)* My life's simply unbearable without a bit of courage.

DOROTHY *(cordially)*. You'll be very welcome.

LION *(lowering his voice)*. I'll help to scare off the wild beasts.

(he beckons the others to come closer) All I've got to do is roar—

(he roars; they all jump and Toto scampers behind the tree stump where he remains cowering).

—and every livin' one of 'em will run away like jack-rabbits!

DOROTHY *(shrewdly)*. It seems to me, they are more cowardly than you are.

LION *(paw to lips)*. Shhh! They are! *(beginning to blubber again)* But that doesn't make me any braver—and until I am, I shall be very unhappy.

DOROTHY *(patting Lion's head)*. There, there! Don't cry. Oz will fix you up, I'm sure of it. Come—let's go.

(Dorothy skips in a circle, counter-clockwise, around the log, singing "Hippity Hop").

DOROTHY.

Hippity Hop to the Wizard of Oz
To send me back to Kansas.

(She stops beside Scarecrow, and points to him).

Brains for you—

(She skips over to Woodman, and points to him).

A heart for him—

(She turns to Lion, and points to him).

And courage for the Lion.

(Now all skip in circle, counter-clockwise, Woodman leading off, singing).

ALL:
Hippity Hop to the Wizard of Oz

To send Dorothy back to Kansas.

(All stop skipping, and point to Scarecrow; Scarecrow points to himself).

DOROTHY, WOODMAN. Brains for you—

LION, SCARECROW   Brains for me—

(All point to Woodman; Woodman points to himself).

DOROTHY, SCARECROW. A heart for him—

LION, WOODMAN   A heart for me—

(All point to Lion; Lion points to himself).

DOROTHY, SCARECROW,
                       And courage for the Lion.
WOODMAN and LION

(All complete the circle, and skip off UL., singing, Woodman leads the way swinging his axe. Scarecrow follows, tripping, falling down, and picking himself up again, in the best of humor. Lion roars, and Dorothy brings up the rear, wagging Lion's tail in rhythm to the tune of the song. Just as she is about to exit, she remembers Toto).

DOROTHY. Oh! We've forgotten Toto!

(She calls and whistles).

Toto! Here, boy! Toto!

(She runs across, back, to the R. and off, returning immediately with Toto at her heels, calling after the others).

Wait for us!

(Dorothy and Toto exit UL.).

CURTAIN

END OF ACT ONE

26

ACT TWO

(The Tin Woodman, Scarecrow, Lion, Dorothy and Toto enter L before the House Curtain. They cross the stage from L. to R., marching to the tune of "Hippity Hop" which they are singing lustily).

ALL:

Hippity Hop to the Wizard of Oz,
> We've reached the Emerald City;
>> The streets are green,
>> The shops are green,
> And also all the houses.

Hippity Hop to the Wizard of Oz,
> We've reached the Emerald Palace;
>> The walls are green,
>> The doors are green,
> And also all the windows.

(All exit R., still singing).

Hippity Hop to the Wizard of Oz,
> To send Dorothy back to Kansas;
>> Brains for you—

(Their voices fade in the distance. After a pause, Toto comes scampering back, sniffs along the floor to the C. opening in the curtain and starts to dig a hole in pantomime. He works away furiously for a while, then squeezes under the curtain).

The House Curtain opens on:

ACT TWO

SCENE 1.

Throne Room in the Palace of Oz.

Entrance UR., with steps leading into the room. At the foot of the steps, a green mat. Bench DR. Hanging above the bench is a large sign which says "No Dogs Allowed." Cabinet UC., back. On top of the cabinet: dinner bell; green box containing green spectacles (at least four pairs). Inside cabinet: over-sized cereal box marked "Bran" in large letters; sewing basket, containing scissors, needle and thread, and paper of pins; heart for Woodman. A large decorated screen is LC., concealing the Throne of Oz. The throne is a large green chair, set on a platform, with decorated backing to hide from view the props used by Oz to impress his visitors. Green sky.

27

As the House Curtain opens, a Doorbell is heard ringing off R. Toto runs up the steps, and barks off through the exit UR. The Doorbell rings again. Toto descends the steps, whining. As he reaches the bottom of the steps, loud snores are heard issuing from behind the screen. Tota pricks up his ears, glances toward the screen, and crosses to it. He pulls himself up to his full height and barks indignantly. A particularly sonorous snore is choked off in its prime, and there is sudden startled silence. After a moment, the head of a Soldier With Green Whiskers appears around the edge of the screen.

SOLDIER *(in a small voice)*. Yes?

(Toto barks and rushes up the steps, then turns irately to Soldier, who blinks at him sleepily. The Doorbell rings long and loud).

(snapping awake). Oh! Oh!

(He comes out from behind the screen, hastily setting his hat straight, and smoothing down his whiskers and coat. His uniform is green, and so is his lovely long beard that falls to his knees. He wears green spectacles).

What's the matter—

(The door bell rings again, and Toto bounds to the top of the steps, pointing off urgently with his paw).

Oh, quite so!

(He starts towards the steps, indeed gets half way up, then recollects something, and runs back behind the screen for his gun, which has green flowers growing out of the barrel. Followed closely through every motion by Toto, he stands at attention, facing front, then wheels smartly on his heels, and ascends the steps with military precision. At the top, he remembers something, and wheels around on Toto).

By the way, how did you get in?

(Toto looks quite innocent, as if to say, "Who, Me?" Without taking his eyes off Toto, the Soldier points to the sign over the bench).

Didn't you see that sign over there?

(The door bell rings again urgently, and Toto gives a ferocious little bark, charging the Soldier into going toward the door. The Soldier takes a few steps, wheels again, sticks out his tongue at Toto, then goes to answer the door. As soon as the Soldier's back is turned, Toto bounds down the steps, jumps up on the bench, and reverses the sign to its blank side. A commotion is heard off UR. Toto sits demurely beside the bench).

(off, in a terrified voice) Oh! Oh! Take that Lion away!

(Lion roars objection. Soldier backs hastily through the entrance

and down the steps, followed by Dorothy. Behind her come Scarecrow and Woodman, holding back Lion).

DOROTHY. He won't hurt you.

(To Lion, slapping him on the nose) Be quiet!

SCARECROW. He's really very friendly.

(To Lion, giving him a shake) Shush, you!

WOODMAN. Don't be afraid.

(To Lion, giving him a shake) Stop it!

(Lion stops roaring, aggrieved. By this time, Soldier is at bottom of steps, Dorothy is on the first step, Scarecrow, Woodman and Lion, on second and third steps).

SOLDIER *(timidly).* Is he—tame?

DOROTHY. Oh, yes. And he's a coward, too.

(Lion begins to blubber).

SOLDIER *(taking a peep at Lion).* Well—if that's the case, he may stay.

(Points to green mat at foot of steps) Wipe your feet, and sit over there.

(He indicates bench DR. As Dorothy wipes her feet and turns to the bench, she catches sight of Toto, who bounds over to her).

DOROTHY *(throwing her arms around Toto's neck).* Oh, Toto, I thought I'd lost you. How did you get in?

SOLDIER. That's what I'd like to know.

(Toto looks modest, scratches his chest, and examines his paw).

No dogs allowed here, you know. It says so.

(Pointing to the sign, he gasps as he finds it blank. Dorothy, following his finger, turns to look at it too).

DOROTHY. What says so?

SOLDIER *(glaring at Toto).* Never mind.

(Toto looks modest, scratches his chest, and examines his paw. Meanwhile, the Lion has wiped his feet and comes and sits on the floor in front of Dorothy. Woodman and Scarecrow wipe their feet and sit on the bench beside Dorothy. Soldier stands RC., facing them).

(clearing his throat importantly) Now, then. Why are you here?

DOROTHY. We've come to see the Wizard of Oz.

SOLDIER *(loftily).* Oh, indeed. Are you sure that Oz will see you?

DOROTHY. Why not?

SOLDIER *(surprised)*. Don't you know?

(Dorothy looks at the others questioningly, and they shake their heads).

DOROTHY *(to Soldier)*. No.

SOLDIER. He never lets any one see him!

DOROTHY *(wonderingly)*. Haven't you seen him?

SOLDIER. Great Green-hosphat, no!

SCARECROW. Doesn't he ever go out?

SOLDIER. Never. He sits all day long on his throne, behind that screen. *(He waves grandly to the screen)*.

WOODMAN. But surely, he—talks to you.

SOLDIER. Oh, yes. And his voice is powerful and terrible. And any one who comes to him on a foolish errand, or out of idle curiosity, he will destroy—instantly!

(Soldier thumps his gun on the floor, and they all jump).

DOROTHY *(rising, crossing to Soldier, earnestly)*. But our errand isn't foolish. It's important. And we've been told that Oz is a good wizard.

SOLDIER. So he is. Now—*(He speaks to include all of them)* why do you want to see him?

SCARECROW *(jumping up and crossing to Soldier, eagerly)*. I want him to give me some brains.

SOLDIER. Oh, Oz can do that easily enough. He has more brains than he needs.

WOODMAN *(rising, crossing to R. of Scarecrow)*. And I want him to give me a heart.

SOLDIER. Oz has a large collection of hearts, all sizes and shapes.

LION *(lifting his head, tearfully, still in a sitting position)*. And I want him to give me courage.

SOLDIER *(crossing to screen)*. Oz keeps a big pot of courage behind his throne. *(Turning)* He'll be glad to give you some. *(To Dorothy)* And what do you want, little girl?

DOROTHY. I want him to send me back to Kansas.

SOLDIER *(nonplussed)*. Where's Kansas?

DOROTHY *(sorrowfully)*. I don't know, but it's my home, and I'm sure it's somewhere.

SOLDIER. Very likely. Well, Oz can do anything, so I suppose he'll find Kansas for you. Make yourselves comfortable, and I'll tell him you're here.

(He clicks his heels twice, salutes, shoulders his gun, and exits DL. For a moment, no one moves; the idea of an impending audience with Oz overwhelms them. Then Dorothy speaks in a whisper).

DOROTHY. He said to make ourselves comfortable.

SCARECROW. Maybe we'd better sit down again, huh?

(Dorothy nods; she and Scarecrow go to the bench and sit).

WOODMAN. I'm going to sit on the stairs.

(He starts up the steps. Halfway up, he suddenly cries out, and looks down at his feet. Dorothy and Scarecrow spring up from the bench; Lion sits up straight).

DOROTHY *(to Woodman)*. What's the matter?

WOODMAN *(unhappily)*. I've stepped on a beetle.

(Dorothy and Scarecrow start up the steps; Lion crosses to foot of step).

DOROTHY. Did you kill it?

WOODMAN *(beginning to weep)*. Yes. *(He sits)* Poor little thing.

DOROTHY *(sitting beside him, consolingly)*. You couldn't help it.

(Scarecrow hovers L. of Woodman, sympathetically. Lion crouches down on bottom step, looking up at Woodman).

WOODMAN. I'm always careful not to hurt any living creature.

(The tears run down his face, and the hinges of his jaw begin to rust. A squeak returns to his voice; he speaks with more and more difficulty).

You people with—'earts——'ave something to—'uide you. 'ut I—'av—'ent—a—'eart. Aw—

(Woodman's mouth stays open, and won't close. He makes frantic motions to Dorothy to oil his jaw, but she doesn't understand. Lion is also puzzled. But Scarecrow runs down to the bench, seizes the oil can from Dorothy's basket, and oils Woodman's jaw. After a moment, Woodman closes his mouth. Everyone heaves a great sigh).

Whew! That'll be a lesson to me——to look before I step.

(Soldier marches on smartly from DL. He halts DC. Dorothy runs to him. The others stand attentively on the steps).

DOROTHY. Well? Will he see us?

SOLDIER. Oh, he'll see you—

(Pleased exclamations from the group).

—though, at first, he said I should send you all packing. Then he asked me what you looked like *(to Dorothy)*—and when I mentioned your silver slippers, he was very much interested. But each of you must see him alone. And each one of you must put on— The Spectacles.

DOROTHY. What spectacles?

SOLDIER. The green spectacles.

(Soldier walks up C. to cabinet, back. Dorothy moves up with him).

DOROTHY. But why do we have to wear green spectacles?

(Soldier opens green box on cabinet, and takes out a pair of green spectacles).

SOLDIER. Because if you didn't the brightness and glory of what you are about to see, would blind you.

(Soldier puts spectacles over Dorothy's eyes. Then he fits spectacles on Lion, Scarecrow and Woodman, explaining as he works).

They're all fitted on by me, for I'm the only optometrist in the entire Emerald City. I am the Official Dispenser of Spectacles, and once I have put them on a person, they don't come off unless I say so. Everybody who lives in the Emerald City wears spectacles day and night. Oz ordered it when the city was built, and the order has never been changed.

SCARECROW. Does Oz wear them?

SOLDIER *(shrugging)*. Who knows?

(Scarecrow joins Dorothy, who is sitting on bench DR. He returns the oil can to the basket. Lion is crouched below the screen, squinting through his spectacles out front. Woodman is having his spectacles fitted on. Gong is struck once off L.) There's the signal. Oz is coming!

(He bustles about) Clear the Throne Room! Everyone out! Except you!

(He points to Dorothy. Dorothy watches her friends disappear, one by one, up the steps; first, Woodman; then Lion; finally Scarecrow).

DOROTHY. Oh, dear!

SOLDIER *(placing Dorothy downstage of steps)*. Stand here.

(Gong is struck twice off L.).

That means Oz is seated on his throne. *(He lays his gun on the cabinet, back. General Lights dim. Toto slides over to Dorothy, and whines softly, pressing his body against her legs).*

DOROTHY. Oh, Toto.

(She stoops and puts her arms around him) Are you afraid?

(Toto barks "No!" with false bravado) I am—terribly. I wonder what he's like. I wonder—

SOLDIER. Shhhhhhh!

(He goes to the screen, and pulls it aside L., so that the throne is revealed and he is concealed. Lights up on throne. In the center of the throne is an enormous Head, with no body, no arms, no legs. From behind the throne comes the sonorous voice of Oz).

OZ. I am Oz, the Great and Terrible. Who are you?

DOROTHY *(fearfully)*. I-I'm Dorothy, the small and meek.

OZ. Why do you seek me?

DOROTHY. I've come to you for help.

OZ. Where did you get the silver slippers?

DOROTHY *(glancing down at her feet)*. Oh, they belonged to the Wicked Witch of the East—before my house fell on her and killed her.

OZ. And where did you get the magic mark on your forehead?

DOROTHY *(touching her forehead)*. That's where the Good Witch of the North kissed me goodbye.

OZ *(sharply)*. What do you want me to do?

DOROTHY *(taking a step toward the throne, beseechingly)*. Please—please send me home to Kansas.

OZ *(demandingly)*. What will you do for me in return?

DOROTHY *(hesitatingly)*. What must I do?

OZ *(in ominous tones)*. Kill the Wicked Witch of the West?

DOROTHY *(wailing)*. How can I do that?

OZ. You killed the Witch of the East.

DOROTHY *(beginning to cry)*. That just happened. I couldn't help it.

OZ *(insistently)*. You wear the silver slippers, and they bear a powerful charm.

DOROTHY. But I don't know what it is.

OZ *(sternly)*. Remember—this witch is wicked, and ought to be killed.

DOROTHY *(sobbing)*. I never killed anything—deliberately—in my life. And even if I wanted to kill the Wicked Witch, how could I? If you can't kill her yourself, how do you expect me to do it?

OZ. I don't know. But until the Wicked Witch is dead, you won't see Kansas again. Now, go!

(Gong is struck off L. Lights fade on throne. Soldier moves screen back into place, concealing throne. General light up. Dorothy accompanied by Toto goes over to the bench, weeping, and sits. Toto puts his head in her lap).

SOLDIER *(brusquely sympathetic).* Here now, none of that, miss. It's the Scarecrow's turn next. You'll have to leave.

(He mounts the steps to the entrance, and calls off R.).

Scarecrow! Oz will see you now.

(Dorothy has risen from the bench sorrowfully; and goes to the foot of the steps, followed mournfully by Toto. Once there, however, Toto perks up with a new idea, and while the soldier is preoccupied with Dorothy, he takes advantage of the opportunity to scurry LC., to investigate the screen. The Soldier has come down the steps briskly, and meets Dorothy at the foot).

Don't be so down-hearted, miss. I daresay Oz is a nicer country than Kansas, anyway.

(But this only brings fresh tears from Dorothy, and the Soldier turns away quickly, only to find Toto snooping around his precious screen. He fixes Toto with a stern eye, and points out to the steps. Toto meekly follows Dorothy. Meanwhile, the Scarecrow has entered and started down the steps. He meets Dorothy half way. Toto maneuvers so as to get behind him).

DOROTHY *(to Scarecrow).* There's no hope for me. Oz won't send me home until I've killed the Wicked Witch of the West—and I can never do that.

(Scarecrow pats her shoulder reassuringly, and she proceeds up the steps, and exits off UR. Scarecrow continues on down the steps to the bottom, with Toto closely in his wake dodging to keep out of the Soldier's sight).

SOLDIER *(suddenly).* Halt!

(Scarecrow stops so quickly that Toto rams against him, and he loses his balance, teetering first this way, and then that, giving Toto an opportunity to scurry across and conceal himself under the bench).

Oh, my goodness! Don't fall!

(But the Scarecrow finally lands in a heap on the floor. The gong sounds twice off L.).

Oz is ready to see you!

(General Lights dim. Scarecrow gets to his feet as best as he can, and steadies his legs under him. Soldier opens the screen back as before, revealing the throne and concealing himself. Lights up on throne. Sitting on the throne is a most lovely Lady. She is dressed in green silk gauze, and wears a crown of jewels upon her long

green hair. In her hand, she holds a sceptre, tipped with the letters "O" and "Z").

SCARECROW *(goggle-eyed).* Ooooooo!

(He snatches off his hat, and bows as prettily as his straw stuffing will allow. The Lady smiles on him sweetly).

OZ *(speaking in a feminine voice).* I am Oz. Who are you?

SCARECROW. I'm a Scarecrow, stuffed with straw.

OZ. What do you want?

SCARECROW *(stuttering with embarrassment).* Well— I-I-I came to ask if y-y-you'd put some b-b-brains in my head.

OZ. Why should I do this for you?

SCARECROW *(smirking).* Well, I—I want to be a man—and no one else can help me.

OZ. I never grant favors without some return.

SCARECROW *(eagerly).* Yes?

OZ. Kill the Wicked Witch of the West, and I shall make you the wisest man in the Land of Oz.

SCARECROW *(surprised).* I thought you asked Dorothy to kill the Witch.

OZ. I did. I don't care who kills her. But until she's dead, you won't get your brains.

SCARECROW *(crestfallen).* Oh-h-h.

OZ. Now, go—and don't come back until you've earned your brains.

(Gong is struck once off L. Lights fade on throne. Soldier moves screen back into place, concealing throne. General Lights up. Scarecrow puts on his hat, turns away sorrowfully, and starts up the steps).

SOLDIER *(arranging the screen, speaks over his shoulder to Scarecrow).* Call the Tin Woodman, there's a good fellow.

(Scarecrow nods, and slowly climbs the steps; at the top, he slips and rolls to the bottom. This happens twice, and he looks at the Soldier, grinning foolishly).

(exasperated) Oh, I'll do it myself! *(He steps over Scarecrow, mounts the steps smartly, and shouts off R.).* *(calling)* Tin Woodman! Tin Woodman!

WOODMAN *(appearing).* Yes, sir?

SOLDIER. Come along! You're next.

(Soldier descends the steps, jumps over Scarecrow, who is still sprawled on the floor, trying to rise. Soldier crosses to the screen,

35

and stands at attention. Woodman hurries down the steps and assists Scarecrow to his feet).

WOODMAN *(in a loud whisper).* What's he like?

SCARECROW *(dejectedly).* He's a Lady—and she needs a heart more than you do.

(Woodman clucks sympathetically, feeling sorry for the Lady. Scarecrow goes up the steps and off R. Gong is struck twice off L. Woodman glances apprehensively toward the screen, then speaks to himself).

WOODMAN. I wonder if Oz will be a Horrible Head or a Lovely Lady. I hope he'll be a Lovely Lady.

(Soldier removes the screen as before. General Lights dim. Woodman squares his shoulders and faces L. Lights up on the throne. This time a Beast sits on the throne. It has a head like a rhinoceros, five long arms and legs, and is covered with thick, wooly hair).

(disappointed) Oh, shucks! It's a good thing I haven't a heart, or I'd be scared to death.

OZ *(roaring).* I am Oz!—the Grrrrreat and Terrrrrrible!

WOODMAN *(simply and directly).* I'm a Woodman, made of tin.

OZ. Why do you bother me?

WOODMAN. I want a heart. I haven't one.

OZ *(growling).* Goooood!

WOODMAN *(staunchly).* It's not good.

(Taking a step toward the throne) I beg you—give me a heart!

OZ. Why?

WOODMAN. I want to be a human being once more.

OZ *(gruffly).* If you want a heart, you must earn it.

WOODMAN. How?

OZ. Help Dorothy kill the Wicked Witch, and I will give you a heart bigger than

(roaring) ALL OZ! GO!

(Gong is struck once off L. Lights fade on throne. Soldier moves screen back into place. General Lights up. Woodman stands glued to the spot, looking hopelessly in front of him. The tears begin to trickle down his cheeks).

WOODMAN *(hastily wiping away his tears).* Oh, dear! I mustn't cry. My jaws will rust again.

(He opens and shuts his jaws vigorously. Soldier jostles against Woodman as he places the screen around the Throne).

SOLDIER. Here now! Get a move on! I can't be shoving this screen around all day. Call the Lion—if you can do it without tumbling downstairs.

(Woodman climbs the steps without mishap. He calls off R.).

WOODMAN. Mr. Lion. It's your turn now.

(Lion enters, a little nervously).

LION *(to Woodman).* What did he look like this time?

WOODMAN. A Beast—a roaring Beast!

LION. Then I'll roar right back at him.

WOODMAN. He roars pretty loud.

LION. I'll roar louder!

WOODMAN. But what if he's a Lovely Lady?

LION. I'll pretend to spring at her.

WOODMAN. And if he's a Horrible Head?

LION. I'll kick it, and roll it around the room, until he promises to give us what we want.

(He pats Woodman on shoulder) Cheer up! Everything's going to be all right.

(Lion marches down the steps. Woodman exits off UR. Gong is struck twice off L. General Lights dim. Soldier moves back the screen. Color Wheel on throne to give the impression of a Ball of Fire. Lion backs away).

OZ *(speaking in a crackling voice).* I am Ozzzzz. Who are you?

LION *(trembling from head to foot).* I'm a c-c-cowardly Lion. I'm af-f-fraid of everything. P-p-please give me some courage.

OZ. Why should I?

LION. Because only you can do it. You're the greatest of all wizards.

OZ. Bring me proof when the Wicked Witch is dead, and I will give you courage.

(Gong is struck once off L. Color Wheel fades on the throne. Soldier moves the screen back into place. General Lights up. Lion suddenly turns tail and rushes up the steps).

SOLDIER *(shouting after him).* Here, here! Come back! There's no need for you to go running off like that. The interviews are over. I'll get the others.

(Soldier goes to the cabinet, picks up his gun and shoulders it.

Lion comes down the steps; Soldier goes up them. Lion tiptoes over to the screen, and tries to peek through a crack).

(calling off UR. You can all come in now. *(Soldier catches sight of Lion peeking through the screen)* Great Green-hosaphat! *(He leaps down the steps)* Get away from there!

(Lion cringes downstage).

LION *(whimpering).* I didn't see nothing.

SOLDIER *(correcting his grammar).* You didn't see anything! The idea! The very idea! *(Referring to Lion's action).*

(Lion begins to blubber. By this time, the others are entering. Dorothy hurries down the steps and over to the Soldier. Scarecrow and Woodman stop on steps).

DOROTHY *(to Soldier).* What is it! What's he done?

SOLDIER *(outraged).* What's he done? He's a peeping-Tom Lion, that's what!

(Lion sniffles) I caught him trying to spy on Oz through that screen.

DOROTHY *(crossing to Lion).* Shame on you!

LION *(weeping).* I just wanted to see the pot of courage he keeps behind his throne. He didn't give me any. He said I'd have to prove the Wicked Witch was dead, first.

DOROTHY *(discouraged).* He told you that, too. Oh, dear! What are we going to do now?

SCARECROW *(crossing to C.).* There's only one thing we can do. Find the Wicked Witch and destroy her.

DOROTHY *(crossing to Scarecrow).* But suppose we can't?

SCARECROW *(sadly).* Then I shall never have any brains.

WOODMAN *(sitting on the steps and sighing).* And I shall never have a heart.

LION *(sitting on the floor, blubbering).* And I shall never have courage.

DOROTHY *(beginning to cry).* And I shall never, never see Aunt Em again.

SOLDIER *(to Dorothy, warningly).* Be careful! Tears will spot your spectacles.

(Dorothy dries her eyes and starts toward the steps. Soldier goes up C. to cabinet during the following dialogue).

DOROTHY. Well, I suppose I can try.

(Stops at foot of steps and turns to Scarecrow).

But I don't want to kill anybody, even to see Aunt Em again.

SCARECROW *(to Dorothy, speaking shyly).* I won't be much help, I'm such a fool, but—I'll go with you.

(Dorothy takes his hand gratefully).

WOODMAN *(springing up).* So will I!

(Goes to Dorothy) Though I haven't the heart to harm even a witch.

(Dorothy links her arm through his, smiling up at him).

LION *(getting up and crossing to C., hangs his head).* If you'll have me, I'd like to go, too. I'll try not to be a coward.

(Dorothy quickly crosses to Lion, and kisses him impulsively on the nose).

DOROTHY. You're not a coward. And we'd love to have you.

(Soldier sets his gun on cabinet, picks up the spectacle box, and comes down to the group).

SOLDIER *(raising his voice).* If you're leaving the Emerald City, kindly return your spectacles.

DOROTHY *(crossing to Soldier and removing her spectacles).* Which road leads to the Wicked Witch of the West?

SOLDIER *(holding out the open box to receive the spectacles).* There's no road.

DOROTHY *(dismayed).* No road?

SOLDIER. No one ever goes that way.

(Dorothy turns to Lion, despairingly. Lion goes to Soldier and removes his spectacles, dropping them into the box).

LION. Then how are we going to find her?

SOLDIER. That will be easy. When she knows you're in the Land of the Winkies, she'll find you.

(Scarecrow is coming over with his spectacles in his hand).

(in a terrifying whisper). She will make you all her slaves!

(Scarecrow, Dorothy and Lion shrink back in a huddle. Woodman cowers. Then Scarecrow steps out and crosses to the Soldier).

SCARECROW *(mysteriously).* Maybe she won't!

(Speaking to Soldier in the same terrifying whisper he used). We're going to kill her!

(It's the Soldier's turn to flinch. Scarecrow drops his spectacles triumphantly into the box).

SOLDIER *(regaining his composure)*. Oh, well, that's different. Nobody has ever killed her before, so I naturally thought she'd made slaves of you.

(Woodman comes forward with his spectacles off).

But be careful! She's wicked and fierce and may not allow you to kill her.

WOODMAN. Which way is the Land of the Winkies?

SOLDIER *(pointing off R.)*. Keep to the West, where the sun sets.

(They all face R., then turn to each other with frightened looks, hesitating. Lion starts to moan).

LION. Ooooooo! If only Oz had given me just a sip of courage.

SOLDIER. If I may suggest—Try singing. There's nothing like a song to give you courage.

DOROTHY *(brightening)*. That's so. All right! I'll begin.

(Dorothy sings to the tune of "A-Hunting We Will Go").

> Oh, to Winkie Land we'll go,
> To Winkie Land we'll go.
> We'll catch a Witch,
> And beat her with a switch,
> And drown her in a ditch, ho, ho!

(Dorothy raises her hand to start the others off).

(holding first note). O-o-o-o-h—

(Scarecrow joins in).

> —to Winkie Land we'll go,
> To Winkie Land we'll go,

(Woodman joins in).

> We'll catch a Witch,
> And beat her with a switch,
> And drown her in a ditch, ho, ho!

(Lion has been plucking up his courage to sing, and now begins with a loud, long, off-key "O-o-o-o-h!" which he sings alone).

LION. O-o-o-o-o-h—

(The others join in, and with Lion leading the way, they march up the steps).

ALL.   —to Winkie Land we'll go,
> To Winkie Land we'll go,
> We'll catch a Witch,
> And beat her with a switch,
> And drown her in a ditch, ho, ho!

(Dorothy crosses to the bench for her basket. She whistles to Toto, who is setting alert, below the bench, waiting for a signal from Dorothy. He bounds to his feet with a bark, and stands ready to follow her, but the Soldier crosses sternly to the bench, and reverses the sign again, then turns and glares pointedly at Toto. Toto takes the hint, and scampers quickly up the steps in pursuit of the rest of the party. Once at the top, however, he turns back, wiggles his ears at the Soldier, then sedately marches off after his friends. The singing continues until all are off, and fades in the distance).

General Lights fade.

The House Curtain closes.

Music Bridges: "A-Hunting We Will Go" (recording), followed by "The Farmer in the Dell."

————

Lights: special spot on L. proscenium arch and steps.

House Curtain opens on:

ACT TWO

SCENE 2.

Land of the Winkies.   Late Afternoon.

Act Curtain is closed. Enter rear of auditorium, Stage left aisle: Woodman, Lion, Dorothy, Scarecrow and Toto, singing. Dorothy's sunbonnet is on her head, shielding her face from the sun.

ALL *(to the tune of "The Farmer in Dell").*

> We've ten miles to go,
> We've ten miles to go,
> We walk a while, we rest a while,
> We've nine miles to go.

(Four verses are sung, subtracting a mile in each verse, until the five-mile point is reached. Dorothy collapses on the Stage Left steps. Woodman and Lion are on the apron; Scarecrow is behind Dorothy; Toto behind Scarecrow, at the foot of the steps).

DOROTHY *(wailing with fatigue).* I can't go another mile!

(The singing stops).

LION *(turning to Dorothy).* But we've only five more to go.

DOROTHY *(rubbing her ankles).* I don't care. I couldn't walk another inch, if Kansas were right around the corner.

41

(Toto sits down on the bottom step. Scarecrow squints up at the spotlight).

SCARECROW. Do you think the sun will ever set? It's been shining overhead since we left the Emerald City.

DOROTHY. I'm so hot and thirsty.

WOODMAN. I'll go look for a spring.

(Woodman starts R., but is brought up short by the sudden entrance of two Winkies, charging him with spears).

WINKIES *(giving their battle-cry).* Scat! Skidaddale! Skidoo!

(They are dressed in yellow: yellow peaked hats, trimmed with a red feather; yellow tunics and tights; yellow Jester slippers with pointed toes. Dorothy screams, Toto barks, Scarecrow yells, Lion roars and Woodman swings his axe. In a moment, the Winkies are surrounded. Scarecrow wrenches the spear from First Winkie; Lion, from Second Winkie. Winkies cower, terrified).

FIRST WINKIE. Don't hurt us!

SECOND WINKIE. We won't harm you!

LION *(roaring).* Tush! You tried to kill us!

SECOND WINKIE. We didn't want to!

FIRST WINKIE. The Wicked Witch made us!

SCARECROW. What Wicked Witch?

FIRST WINKIE. The Wicked Witch of the West!

(General reaction on the part of the others).

SECOND WINKIE. She said, "Go to those people, and stab them to pieces!"

FIRST WINKIE. We had to obey her. We're her slaves.

(Dorothy has crept up the steps, with Toto. Toto remains by L. proscenium arch. Dorothy crosses to Scarecrow.

DOROTHY *(to Winkies).* Are we in the Land of the Winkies?

WINKIES *(nodding).* Yes, Miss.

DOROTHY. How did the Witch know we were here?

SECOND WINKIE. She could see you coming with her one eye.

(Winkie points to his right eye) It's as powerful as a telescope, and can see everywhere.

FIRST WINKIE. She was so angry, she tore her hair.

(Imitates Witch tearing her hair).

DOROTHY *(shrinking back).* Oh-h-h.

(Scarecrow puts his arm around Dorothy protectingly. Woodman steps forward and speaks to Winkies).

WOODMAN. Can she see what's happening here right now?

SECOND WINKIE *(shuddering).* Oh, yes—and we'll get a terrible beating.

DOROTHY *(crossing between Winkies, protesting).* She shan't beat you! I won't let her.

FIRST WINKIE. You can't stop her. You're just a little girl.

LION. Then I will!

WOODMAN. And I!

SCARECROW. All of us will! There are—

(counting and adding up on his fingers)—four of us!

FIRST WINKIE *(desperately).* Four thousand—four hundred thousand couldn't stop the Wicked Witch. She'll send her pack of wolves to tear you to pieces, and her wild crows to peck your eyes out! She'll send her black bees to sting you to death! And then she'll—

SECOND WINKIE *(suddenly holding up his hand).* Listen!

(A hush falls over the group as they strain their ears to listen. A low distant whirring sound is heard in the air).

DOROTHY *(stepping forward).* What's that noise?

SCARECROW *(looking around, puzzled).* Where's it coming from?

(The two Winkies have turned their eyes R. front).

SECOND WINKIE *(pointing).* Look! Look up there!

(There is a rushing of many wings, a great chattering and laughing, and the sky darkens. Lights dim).

FIRST WINKIE. It's the Winged Monkeys!

SECOND WINKIE. The Witch has sent her Winged Monkeys to kill us!

FIRST WINKIE. Run for your lives!

(The noise becomes deafening. Lightning flashes. There is a mad dash for safety, as first the Winkies, then Dorothy, Toto, Scarecrow, Woodman and Lion scramble for the exit L. The din lessens and finally subsides).

Act Curtain opens on:

ACT TWO

SCENE 3.

Court yard of the Yellow Castle. Evening.

Black Traveller closed. Well, L. Wooden pail and scrubbing brush beside well. Stool, R. Curtained cupboard, R.C., back. Inside cupboards Golden Cap; loaf of bread, cheese and apples. Leaning against cupboard, broom of twigs. Lights: eerie, yellow predominating; UC, back, dim, to facilitate "melting" of Witch through curtain. Witch of the West is discovered, L. of stool, hopping on her left foot, supporting herself on a purple umbrella. She is dressed in a full brown cloak, with wide sleeves, that opens down the back; green under-dress and stockings; black shoes with buckles; and a peaked brown hat. Her hair is gray and scraggly, and she wears a black patch over her left eye.

WITCH OF THE WEST *(chanting and hopping on left foot).*

> Ep-pe- pep-pe, kak-ke!
> Ep-pe- pep-pe, kak-ke!

(Hopping on right foot).

> Hil-lo, hol-lo, hel-lo!
> Hil-lo, hol-lo, hel-lo!

(She repeats the chant again, then jumps on both feet, and exclaims).

Ziz-zy, zuz-zy, zik!

(During the Witch's chanting, Dorothy, First and Second Winkies enter DL. They stop nervously downstage of the well. Dorothy has lost her sunbonnet, but is still clutching the basket. Witch catches sight of them, turns, and lets out a bellow of rage. She shakes her umbrella at the Winkies, who instinctively raise their arms to ward off the blows they expect to receive. But the Witch stands C. and flourishes her umbrella at them instead).

Sooooo!—you yellow Jackanapes! You've come back at last, have you? Why didn't you carry out my orders, eh?

FIRST WINKIE *(stuttering with fright).* We d-d-didn't have time! The Monkeys—

WITCH OF THE WEST. Don't lie to me, you saffron rascals! I saw everything with my one eye. Where's the Lion?

SECOND WINKIE *(points off L).* He's tied up in the thistle patch behind the iron fence.

WITCH OF THE WEST *(turning away and twirling her umbrella like a whip).* I'll harness him like a horse, to pull my carriage.

44

(Suddenly she whirls on the Winkies) And the men of tin and straw?

FIRST WINKIE. The Tin Man was dropped on the rocks by the Winged Monkeys, and the Straw Man had all his straw pulled out of him.

(Witch advances on Dorothy, pointing with her umbrella).

WITCH OF THE WEST. Why wasn't this girl made an end of, too?

(Dorothy screams, and darts past Witch to R., putting the stool between them).

FIRST WINKIE *(with a trace of triumph in his voice).* The Monkeys didn't dare to hurt her.

WITCH OF THE WEST *(fiercely).* Why not?

FIRST WINKIE. She's protected by the Power of Good.

WITCH OF THE WEST *(moving toward Dorothy, scornfully).* In what way?

FIRST WINKIE *(crossing to Witch).* The mark of the Good Witch's kiss is on her forehead.

WITCH OF THE WEST *(crying out and recoiling).* No!

(Winkies break into jeering laughter. Witch turns on them furiously).

(shrieking) Get out! Go back to your furnaces and your hammers and anvils, and make me the finest gold horseshoes in the kingdom for the Lion, or by the black beard of my grandmother, I'll have the skin off your backs! Go!

(Winkies exit DL. in haste. Witch turns to Dorothy who is cowering behind the stool. She points to the pail and scrubbing brush beside the well).

(harshly) Scrub the courtyard! I'm going for a drive, and the Lion shall be my horse!

(She exits DL., cackling. Left alone, Dorothy sits on the stool, sets her basket on the floor, and begins to cry).

DOROTHY. I'll never get back to Kansas and Aunt Em now. I wonder what happened to Toto. I suppose they killed him, too.

(She sobs bitterly. At this moment, Toto comes out from behind the well, and crawls on tiptoe to Dorothy, unobserved by her. He stands upon his hind legs behind her, and taps her on the left shoulder. Immediately he steps lightly to R. of her. She is startled by the tap, and looks fearfully over her left shoulder. Seeing no one there, she faces front again, puzzled. Toto taps her right shoulder, and steps quickly to L. Dorothy looks over her right shoulder, and Toto covers her eyes with his paws).

(timidly) Who is it?

(She feels Toto's paws, and exclaims joyfully) Toto, Oh, Toto!

(Toto barks and she jumps to her feet and embraces him). You're safe! You're alive! Oh, Toto!

(Suddenly, off L., there is a tremendous roar from the Lion, mingled with screams of pain from the Witch).

(Hustling Toto DR.) Quick. The Witch is coming! Hide! Hide!

(She pushes Toto to DR. steps, and he crouches behind them. Dorothy then runs to the well, and snatches up the scrubbing brush. She dips it in the pail, gets down on her hands and knees, and begins to scrub like mad. Witch enters DL., limping and rubbing her thigh. She crosses to the stool).

WITCH OF THE WEST *(snarling).* That beast has bitten me! Well, if I can't harness him, I can starve him.

(She sits on the stool) He shall have nothing to eat until he does as I say.

(Dorothy springs to her feet, and still holding the scrubbing brush, runs over to Witch).

DOROTHY *(protesting).* Don't starve him!

(At sight of the scrubbing brush in Dorothy's hand, the Witch leaps backward from the stool, giving a loud cry of fear).

WITCH OF THE WEST. Aaaaaah! Don't touch me! Don't touch me with that scrubbing brush! Take it away! There's water on it! Don't you know that water would be the end of me?

(She threatens Dorothy with her umbrella) Idiot!

(Dorothy steps back hastily to avoid being hit, and in doing so, one of her slippers twists on her foot. She stoops over to put it straight again, and the Witch looks down at Dorothy's feet. She sucks in her breath, and speaks in a hoarse whisper).

(Pointing) Where did you get those slippers?

DOROTHY *(straightening up).* The Good Witch gave them to me.

WITCH OF THE WEST. They didn't belong to her.

DOROTHY *(boldly).* They didn't belong to you, either.

WITCH OF THE WEST *(pounding the floor with her umbrella).* Hold your tongue!

(Points off R) Now, go down cellar and bring me the jar of snake-oil you'll find under the stairs.

(Dorothy hesitates) And be quick about it!

(Dorothy puts the scrubbing brush beside the pail).

46

DOROTHY *(faltering)*. Snake-oil?

WITCH OF THE WEST. Aye!

DOROTHY. What's it for?

WITCH OF THE WEST *(testily)*. What would it be for?—but to rub on the place where the Lion bit me, you booby!

(Witch rubs her thigh, and Dorothy looks hard at it).

DOROTHY. But it's not bleeding.

WITCH OF THE WEST *(thumping her umbrella on the floor)*. Do as you're told!

(Dorothy skirts the Witch neatly, and exits R. Witch gazes after her, cunningly, then speaks to herself).

If only I could get hold of those silver slippers! She's such a simple soul, she doesn't know their magic.

(She crosses up to the cupboard) They would give me more power than everything else.

(She draws back the cupboard curtain and takes out the Golden Cap from the shelf, admiring it) More power even than the Gold Cap.

(She returns the Cap to the cupboard shelf, and closes the curtain) I must try to get them. I must!

(She crosses down to LC.) But how! How! A trick—my umbrella for a trick.

(She stops short) Umbrella.

(Looks at umbrella; an idea begins to take form) Of course! Just the thing!

(She crosses R.) I'll put it here, and make it invisible.

(She places the umbrella on the floor before R. entrance) She'll trip over it, and when she falls—I'll snatch the slippers from her feet.

(She cocks her ear R., and rubs her palms together in high spirits. Then she jumps on both feet, extends her arms above the umbrella and chants vigorously).

Ziz-zy, zuz-zy, zik!

(She crosses UR., awaiting developments. Dorothy enters, carrying an earthenware jar. She stumbles over the umbrella and falls full length. With lightning speed, the Witch darts downstage, and grabs one of the silver slippers from Dorothy's foot, but is prevented from getting the other by Toto, who dashes out of hiding to confront the Witch, barking ferociously).

Where did this beast come from? Call him off.

(Dorothy scrambles to her feet, and the Witch retreats up RC. with the slipper).

DOROTHY *(angrily).* Give me my slipper!

WITCH OF THE WEST *(laughing maliciously).* He, he! It's my slipper, now! And some day, I'll get the other one, too.

DOROTHY *(advancing on her).* You wicked thing! You've no right to take my slipper.

WITCH OF THE WEST. I shall keep it, just the same. He, he!

(Chuckling, the Witch circles R. and downstage of the stool, crossing to the well, to avoid Dorothy, who follows her, trying to retrieve her slipper. In a rage, Dorothy picks up the pail of water beside the well, and dashes it over the Witch, wetting her from head to foot.

The Witch gives a loud shriek, and staggers upstage to C. of black traveller, so that her back is to the opening. Then she begins to "melt" through the curtain).

(In agony) See what you've done! Soon there'll be nothing left of me.

DOROTHY. I'm very sorry.

WITCH OF THE WEST *(wailing).* No, you're not! You knew that water would be the end of me.

DOROTHY *(distressed).* But I didn't know you'd melt, like brown sugar.

WITCH OF THE WEST *(despairingly).* In a minute, I shall have melted all away. And the Castle will be yours. All my evil work is undone, now that my power is going. I've been wicked in my day, but I never thought a little girl like you would be able to melt me, and end my wicked deeds. Look out! Here I go!

(With a low moan, the Witch disappears through the curtain, and only her cloak and hat remain, lying in a heap on the floor. Dorothy goes over and holds the apparel up in wide-eyed wonder).

DOROTHY. I can't believe it! She's really melted. Melted clean away.

(She drops the cloak and hat on the stool, picks up her silver slipper, and puts it on).

(excitedly) Toto! We've done it! We've done it! We've destroyed The Wicked Witch! For ever and ever. And we can go back to Kansas!

(Toto leaps up the steps, barking, and does a "Ring-around-the-Rosy" with Dorothy).

(pushing him L.) **Run, and let the Lion out!** And tell the Win-kies they're free!

(Toto capers off DL., Dorothy crosses to the stool and picks up her basket).

I'll fill my basket with food from the Witch's cupboard.

(She crosses up to the cupboard and draws back the curtain. She sees the Golden Cap).

(delighted) Oh! What an odd little hat!

(She takes it from the shelf) I'd like to try it on.

(She lifts it to her head, then hesitates) Why not?

(She puts it on) It fits!

(Gaily) I'll wear it.

(She packs her basket with bread, cheese and apples, and is just turning away from the cupboard, when Lion enters DL. with a roar of joy. He gallops toward Dorothy, she sets her basket in the cupboard, and runs to him. They meet C. and embrace).

LION *(roaring)*. Soooooo! The Wicked Witch is destroyed! I'm glad I got to bite her before she melted away. You know, she didn't bleed at all. She was all dried up!

(A triumphant barking is heard off L. and Toto enters DL. sedately, leading a small procession, consisting of:

First and Second Winkies, with Madame Winkie, who is in yellow, like the men: yellow dress, apron and bonnet. She wears spectacles, and a large needle, threaded with a long piece of twine, is stuck in the bosom of her dress.

The three Winkies cheer, and join hands, dancing around Dorothy and Lion. After two or three times around, they break the ring, Toto barks for attention and First Winkie makes a speech. It's the first public speech of his life, and the importance of it weighs heavily on his mind).

FIRST WINKIE *(declaiming)*. On behalf of the Winkie citizens of this Yellow Country, I thank you for delivering us from the Wicked Witch. We rejoice that we are no longer her slaves. This day shall be kept as a holiday, now and ever after.

SECOND WINKIE *(tossing his hat in the air)*. Hip, hip—

MADAME and FIRST WINKIE. Hooray!

SECOND WINKIE. Hip, hip—

MADAME and FIRST WINKIE. Hooray.

SECOND WINKIE. Hip, hip—

THREE WINKIES. Hooray!

LION *(wistfully)*. If only the Scarecrow and Tin Woodman were here.

(Dorothy appeals to the Winkies).

DOROTHY. Do you suppose you could help our friends?

FIRST WINKIE. We'll try. Where are they?

DOROTHY. The Woodman is lying on a rocky plain, all battered and bent. Are any of your people tinsmiths?

SECOND WINKIE. I am a tinsmith—a very good one, too.

DOROTHY *(crossing to him)*. Could you straighten out the Woodman, and bend him back into shape again? And solder him together where he's broken.

SECOND WINKIE *(confidently)*. I can make him as good as new.

FIRST WINKIE. What about the Scarecrow?

DOROTHY *(turning to him)*. He was tossed into the branches of a tall tree, after his stuffing was pulled out.

FIRST WINKIE *(shaking his head and clucking sympathetically)*. Tch, tch! We must try to find him.

(Madame Winkie speaks for the first time. She crosses to Dorothy and indicates the Golden Cap on her head).

MADAME WINKIE. Why don't you use the charm of the Golden Cap to restore your friends to you?

DOROTHY *(surprised)*. I didn't know there was a charm. What is it?

MADAME WINKIE. It's written inside. It will call the Winged Monkeys to you, and they'll find your friends, and bring them here in next to no time.

DOROTHY *(anxiously)*. Won't they hurt me?

MADAME WINKIE. Oh, no! They must obey the wearer of the Cap.

FIRST WINKIE *(starting L.)*. I'll get fresh straw to stuff the Scarecrow with.

(Exit DL).

MADAME WINKIE *(taking the needle from the front of her dress and knotting the end of the thread)* I'll sew him up.

SECOND WINKIE *(following First Winkie L.)*. I'll mend the Woodman, and get his joints in working order.

(Exit DL).

(Dorothy has taken off the Cap, and is turning it in her hands apprehensively).

MADAME WINKIE *(giving her a pat, and crossing L.)*. Don't be afraid, ducky. Just follow the directions inside.

(Exit DL).

LION *(coming down to Dorothy)*. What does it say?

(Dorothy looks inside the Cap, and reads the directions carefully out loud).

DOROTHY *(reading)*. Ep-pe, pep-pe, kak-ke.

LION *(nonplussed)*. What'd you say?

DOROTHY. Hil-lo, hol-lo, hel-lo.

LION *(as if answering to a greeting)*. Hello.

DOROTHY. Ziz-zy, zuz-zy, zik!

LION. Sounds like nonsense.

DOROTHY *(putting on the Cap)*. Maybe it is. But I'm going to try it.

(She holds on to the Lion for support and hops on her left foot. Lights begin to dim).

(Chanting) Ep-pe, pep-pe, kak-ke!

Ep-pe, pep-pe, kak-ke!

(Hopping on her right foot) Hil-lo, hol-lo, hel-lo!

Hil-lo, hol-lo, hel-lo!

(She repeats the chanting and hopping a second time, then jumps on both feet) Ziz-zy, zuz-zy, zik!

(Dorothy and Lion listen intently for a moment).

(To Lion) Do you hear anything?

LION *(shaking his head)*. No. Are you sure you did it right?

(Dorothy takes off the Golden Cap, and quickly runs through the directions again, the Lion looking over her shoulder).

LION. You did what it says to do.

DOROTHY *(examining the shape of the Cap)*. Maybe I had it on backwards.

LION. How can you tell? It looks the same all around to me.

DOROTHY *(replacing the Cap on her head)*. Well, I must have done something wrong. I'll try it again.

(She is just about to hop on her left foot, when the distant flapping of wings and chattering is heard).

LION *(lifting his head)*. Wait a minute! I hear something.

51

DOROTHY *(after listening)*. It's the Winged Monkeys all right.

(The sound increases in volume, until it is right overhead and deafening. Dorothy and Lion cover their ears, and duck DR.

Blackout. Dorothy screams. Lion roars. There is a blinding flash behind the well. Flashpot. The Scarecrow is revealed, standing UC. between First Winkie and Madame Winkie. The Tin Woodman is standing downstage of the well with the Second Winkie. First Winkie is stuffing straw up Scarecrow's sleeve, and Madame Winkie is sewing his shoulder. Second Winkie is holding soldering iron to Woodman's knee joint. Lights come up quickly on scene. Sound of Winged Monkeys dies away).

(Dorothy and Lion exclaim with joy at the sight of their two friends, alive and whole again and Toto barks and gambols with glee. They rush to embrace them. General rejoicing: Woodman weeps with emotion, and Dorothy carefully wipes away his tears, and then her own with her handkerchief).

You mustn't cry. You'll rust your joints.

(Lion also weeps, wiping his eyes with the tip of his tail and wringing it out afterwards. Scarecrow pulls a bit of straw from his sleeves and blows his nose on it. Meantime, the Winkies stand by, beaming. Scarecrow suddenly sees the Witch's cloak and hat on the stool; he holds them up).

SCARECROW *(curiously)*. What's this?

DOROTHY *(laughing, going to him)*. It's all that's left of the Wicked Witch. She melted right out of them!

SCARECROW *(jubilantly, dropping the Witch's attire back on the stool)*. Now we can go back to Oz, and I'll get my brains!

WOODMAN *(joyfully)*. And I'll get a heart!

LION *(pounding his chest)*. And I'll get courage!

DOROTHY *(clapping her hands)*. And I can go home to Kansas! Let's start for the Emerald City now!

LION *(stopping Dorothy)*. Wait a minute!

(Uneasily) What way shall we go? There's no road—remember?

DOROTHY *(logically)*. When we came here, we went straight west, toward the setting sun. So now, we'll go straight east, toward the rising sun.

SCARECROW *(philosophically)*. If we walk far enough. we're bound to come to some place, you know.

(General laughter).

FIRST WINKIE *(stepping forward)*. We're sorry to have you leave us.

(Dorothy crosses to First Winkie and shakes hands with him).

DOROTHY *(warmly)*. We owe our lives to you. If it hadn't been for you Winkies, we just wouldn't be here—especially the Scarecrow and Tin Woodman.

SECOND WINKIE *(crossing to Woodman)*. We'd like you to stay, and be our King.

WOODMAN *(honored)*. Oh, thank you! You're very kind.

(Sadly) But I'm afraid I wouldn't make a good King, without a heart.

SECOND WINKIE. Then, will you promise to come back to us, after Oz has given you a heart?

WOODMAN. Oh, yes—if you still want me.

SECOND WINKIE *(positively)*. We'll want you.

FIRST WINKIE *(shouting)*. The Witch is dead! Long live the King!

(Everyone cheers, and the cheering resolves into singing. A circle is formed around the stool holding the Witch's cloak and hat, and to the tune of "Here We Go Round the Mulberry Bush", the group sings the following stanzas, suiting the action to the words).

ALL *(singing and circling clockwise)*.
    Here we go round the Wicked Witch,
    The Wicked Witch, the Wicked Witch,
    Here we go round the Wicked Witch,

(Group stops circling, and Dorothy holds up the Witch's cloak and hat).

DOROTHY. At least as much as is left of her!

(General laughter. In the next verse, on the word "melted", everyone collapses to the floor, in place, then straightens up on the words "briney salt", reading to collapse a second time).

ALL. She melted away like briney salt,
    Briney salt, briney salt,
    Melted away like briney salt,
    And we are very glad of it.

(Everyone claps hands and leaps into the air on the word "glad". Group now circles counter-clockwise).

WINKIES. They're going to claim their just reward.

OTHERS. We're going to claim our just reward,

ALL. Just reward, just reward,
    Going to claim their just reward,
    Going to claim our just reward,
(Group stops circling).

ALL. From Oz, the Wonderful Wizard.

(Scarecrow walks clockwise, in character, around the outside of the circle and back to place).

SCARECROW. He promised me a set of brains,
Set of brains, set of brains,
Promised me a set of brains,

ALL. Did Oz, the Wonderful Wizard.

(Woodman walks counter-clockwise, in character, around the outside of the circle and back to place).

WOODMAN. He promised me a loving heart,
Loving heart, loving heart,
Promised me a loving heart,

ALL. Did Oz, the Wonderful Wizard.

(Lion walks clockwise, in character, around the outside of the circle and back to place).

LION. He promised to fill me full of courage,
Full of courage, full of courage,
Promised to fill me full of courage,

ALL. Oz, the Wonderful Wizard.

(Dorothy skips counter-clockwise around the outside of the circle and back to place).

DOROTHY. He promised to send me back to Kansas,
Back to Kansas, back to Kansas,
Promised to send me back to Kansas,

ALL. Oz, the Wonderful Wizard.

(All, except Winkies, exit in single file DL., Dorothy leading).

And so, goodbye, and thank you all,
Thank you all, thank you all,
So, goodbye, and thank you all,
We'll never forget your kindness.

(Fade in recording of "Here We Go Round the Mulberry Bush"; play to end scene).

WINKIES *(in chorus, waving).* Goodbye! Goodbye!

(First and Second Winkies continue to wave. Madame Winkie turns to stool, picks up the Witch's cloak and hat, and crosses up to the cupboard to put them away. Pulling back the curtain, she notices Dorothy's basket on the shelf, and gives an exclamation of dismay. Winkies hear her and turn questioningly).

MADAME WINKIE *(holding up the basket).* She's forgotten her basket of food—and the Woodman's oil can!

54

(There is a series of sharp barks off DL., and Toto comes bound-ing on-stage. He knocks over First Winkie and barely misses bowling over the Second Winkie. Rushing up to Madame Winkie, he takes the basket in his mouth, and dashes back to the exit DL. First Winkie is just getting to his feet, and Toto knocks him down a second time as:—the House Curtain closes.

END OF ACT TWO

ACT THREE

Scene 1.

Throne Room in the Palace of Oz.

Everything is the same as in ACT TWO: Scene 1, except that the sign "NO DOGS ALLOWED" is hanging now on the screen in front of the throne. The Soldier is on the bench DR., asleep and snoring as usual, with his head upstage, and his hat covering his face. His gun is propped against his legs, downstage of the bench.

Toto enters stealthily UR., looking back over his shoulder as if he is afraid of being caught. He doesn't see the Soldier, who has stopped snoring momentarily. Toto turns and his eye catches the sign on the screen. He descends the steps and goes over to it. He stands on his hind legs and reads the sign, snorting contemptuously. He lifts the sign off the nail just as the soldier gives a tremendous snore. Toto whirls about, dropping on all fours, and growls his vexation: "Sleeping again!"

Toto gets an idea, tiptoes over to the soldier, and carefully, so as not to disturb him, removes his hat from his face and hangs the sign around his neck, lifting the Soldier's long green whispers over the string and letting the cardboard rest on the floor behind the soldier.

Sound: Bell rings off UR. The soldier doesn't stir. Toto tickles his nose with his paw. The Soldier twitches a little. Toto tickles his nose again. The Soldier mumbles and brushes away Toto's paw with his hand. He turns over and settles down more comfortably.

Sound: Bell rings off UR. Toto makes an impatient movement, and looks around the room for some other means of waking up the Soldier. He notices the dinner bell on the cabinet UC., back. He gets it, returns to the Soldier, and rings the bell directly above his head.

The Soldier awakens with a start; his gun clatters to the floor, and he hasn't quite collected his wits, when he catches sight of Toto, doubled up with laughter).

SOLDIER *(standing up, trying to regain his equilibrium)*. Greenhosaphat! Are you back again. Can't you read the sign?

(He totters over to the screen, pointing).

TOTO *(barking innocently)*. What sign?

SOLDIER *(confused at finding the sign gone)*. The sign— The sign—

(He rubs his eyes) Up to your old tricks again, eh?

(Of course it is dangling down behind him, but he is too flustered to notice).

56

There was a sign here. I made it myself.

(He speaks with exasperation and, seeing the dinner bell in Toto's paw, he snatches it away, stomping up to the cabinet with it).

I thought you'd gone to visit the Wicked Witch of the West.

TOTO *(barking).* We did.

SOLDIER *(coming down to Toto, amazed).* And she let you go?

(Toto pantomimes the Witch melting away).

(Gasping) Melted away? Who melted her?

(Toto barks the name, "Dorothy").

(Overawed) Dorothy? Great Green-hosaphat!

(Sound: Bell rings again, this time long and loud. The Soldier is startled into sudden activity. He rushes to the bench, collecting his hat and gun every which way).

(Excitedly) I must tell the Colonel, and the Captain, and the Corporal, and the Corporal's wife, and his wife's father's wife, and she'll tell everyone else in the city!

(He makes a mad dash for the steps, his hat awry, his gun shouldered upside down. Suddenly he stops in his headlong ascent of the steps and turns to Toto).

(Speaking deliberately) Listen, there is a penalty for removing state property.

(Toto sits at the foot of the steps and laughs derisively, wiggling his ears).

I must go look it up in the book.

(He continues up the steps and off UR).

Got to tell the Colonel, and the Captain, and the Corporal, and the Corporal's wife—

(He is out of earshot. Toto scrambles up the steps to greet his friends, barking them in. Dorothy, Scarecrow, Woodman, and Lion enter UR. Scarecrow is carrying Dorothy's basket. She is wearing the Golden Cap. She sees Toto and goes to him).

DOROTHY *(surprised).* Toto! What are you doing here?

(Soldier reappears UR., hustles down the steps and up back to the cabinet. He sets down his gun).

SOLDIER. He's broken the law, that's what he's done, but I have to get the book and look it up.

(He takes up the box of green spectacles, and crosses down to Dorothy) Now, here. Put on the green spectacles at once. Dorothy, you pass them out.

(He goes to the screen) I'll move the screen.

(He does so, while Dorothy distributes the spectacles. When she is finished, she returns the box to the cabinet. Toto decides to explore and trots DL., glancing back to make sure his exit won't be noticed. He exits DL).

(Keeping up a steady stream of comment as he arranges the screen) Oz will just have to see you all at the same time today. I'm in a green-hosaphat of a hurry! Such news!

(He gets tangled up in the sign "NO DOGS ALLOWED" that Toto has hung backwards around his neck, and he removes it, without realizing immediately what it is. Then he recognizes it).

(With wonder) Why, here it is! Now, how did—

(Quickly hanging it back on the screen) Oh, never mind! I haven't time. I've got to tell them all about it. I'll let Oz know you're here.

(He starts DL., counting off on his fingers) The Colonel, the Captain, the Corporal, the Corporal's wife, his wife's father's wife—

(He stops DL., rapidly checking off five fingers, nods in agreement, and exits with a flourish of the hand) And she'll tell every one else in the city!

(Dorothy turns around, expecting Toto is somewhere behind her).

DOROTHY. Now, Toto, please explain—

(She discovers he is gone. There is a general scurrying about, whistling and searching. Everyone speaks together).

SCARECROW *(setting Dorothy's basket on the cabinet and looking under it)* Toto! Come here, you naughty dog!

WOODMAN *(climbing the steps).* Where has he got to? Toto!

LION *(looking under the bench).* Here, boy! Here, boy!

DOROTHY. He was standing right here a minute ago! Toto!

(She snaps her fingers and whistles. Presently, above the tumult, is heard the tremendous voice of Oz).

OZ *(thundering).* QUIET!

(Everybody stops dead in his tracks, silenced).

What's all the hullabaloo about?

DOROTHY *(trying to locate the voice, timidly).* Where are you?

OZ. I am everywhere!

(The others look around the room nervously, moving in behind Dorothy).

Why have you come back to pester me?

(Dorothy fixes her gaze on the throne, although there is nothing there).

DOROTHY.   Please, sir—wherever you are—we've come to ask you to keep your promises to us.

OZ.   What promises?

DOROTHY *(reminding him)*. You promised to send me home to Kansas when the Wicked Witch was destroyed.

SCARECROW.   And you promised to give me brains.

WOODMAN.   And me, a heart.

LION.   And me, courage.

OZ *(after a pause, his voice trembling a little)*. Is the Wicked Witch really destroyed?

DOROTHY.   Yes. I melted her with a bucket of water.

OZ.   Dear me! What a wet end!

DOROTHY *(agreeing)*. Oh, yes, sir!

OZ.   Well, come back tomorrow. I must have time to think it over.

WOODMAN *(angrily)*. You've had plenty of time already!

SCARECROW.   We shan't wait a day longer.

DOROTHY *(insistent)*. You must keep your promises!

(And now Toto proclaims his whereabouts, barking and growling behind the backing of the throne. Intermingled with the canine ejaculations are muffled commands from Oz).

Shoo! Shoo! Go 'way! Nice doggy, Scram!

(Toto apparently pays not the slightest attention, but rather, increases the volume of his barking, and Oz raises the pitch of his outcries, until, at the peak of the uproar, he backs into sight around the upstage edge of the backing, and leaps agilely onto the throne, clutching his trousers around his legs, much as a woman does her skirts).

(In a terrified squeak) Don't you bite me, you brute!

(Toto follows Oz around the backing, yipping like a terrier and enjoying the situation immensely. Having accomplished his mission, which was to force Oz into the open, he bounds DL., and sits against the L. proscenium arch.

The others are standing stock-still in amazement, staring at Oz. He is a little old man, with a bald head and a wrinkled face, who seems to be as much surprised as they are. He is dressed in a Prince Albert coat; striped pegged trousers and gaiters; stand-up collar and cravat. A handkerchief hangs out of his pocket, and there's a flower in his buttonhole).

DOROTHY *(sharply).* Who are you?

OZ *(almost in a whisper, his voice quavering).* I am Oz, the Great and Terrible.

WOODMAN *(raising his axe in indignation).* What!

(Scarecrow and Lion move to Woodman, controlling him).

OZ *(shrinking back).* Oh-oh, don't chop me!

DOROTHY *(dismayed).* You are Oz! But I thought you were a great Head!

SCARECROW.   A lovely Lady!

WOODMAN *(speeches overlapping).* A terrible Beast!

LION.   A Ball of Fire!

OZ *(getting down from the throne, meekly).* No—you're all wrong. I've been—making believe.

(Dorothy and the others gasp).

DOROTHY *(Crying out).* Making believe! Aren't you a Wizard?

OZ. Shhhh! Don't speak so loud! Somebody'll hear you!

(he looks about, petrified) I'm supposed to be a Great Wizard.

DOROTHY *(wailing).* And you're not?

OZ. Shhhh! No. I'm just a common man.

SCARECROW *(coming forward, in a grieved tone).* You're more than that. You're a humbug!

OZ *(rubbing his hands together, pleased).* Exactly! I'm a humbug.

WOODMAN. But this is terrible!

(Turning to Lion).

How shall I ever get my heart?

LION *(to Woodman).* Or I, my courage.

SCARECROW *(turning to Woodman).* Or I, my brains?

OZ *(holding up his hands to calm them).* My dear friends, these are little things. Think of me, and the trouble I'm in, at being found out.

DOROTHY. Doesn't anyone else know you're a humbug?

OZ *(shaking his head).* No one knows it but you four—and myself. It was a great mistake, my ever letting you into the Throne Room.

DOROTHY *(bewildered)*. But I don't understand. How could you appear to us as a Head, and a Ball of Fire, and—

OZ *(interrupting)*. Tricks, my dear. Stage props.

SCARECROW *(crossing to Oz)*. That Lady was no prop!

OZ *(smiling)*. It was me—inside a dress and a mask.

SCARECROW *(turning away, disappointed)*. Aw, heck!

WOODMAN. Really, you ought to be ashamed of yourself.

OZ *(sorrowfully)*. I am—I certainly am.

(He sits on the throne dejectedly) But what else could I do!

DOROTHY. Well, what else did you do, before you came to the Emerald City?

OZ. I'll tell you. Sit down.

(Lion goes and sits on the bench. Woodman and Scarecrow sit on the steps. Dorothy sits on the platform of the throne. When they are all seated, Oz begins).

I was a balloonist with a circus—

DOROTHY. A What?

OZ. A balloonist—a man who goes up in a balloon on circus day.

DOROTHY. Oh! Where?

OZ. In Omaha.

DOROTHY *(delighted)*. Why, that's not far from Kansas!

OZ *(solemnly)*. No, it isn't.

(Sighing) But it's farther from here. Well, one day the balloon drifted away. When it came down, I found myself in this country. The strange people here, seeing me come from the clouds, thought I was a great Wizard. Of course, I let them think so. And because the country was so lovely, I called it the Emerald City. I put green spectacles on all the people so that everything they saw was green.

DOROTHY. Oh, so that's the reason for wearing these spectacles.

OZ *(with an embarrassed sigh)*. Yes. You may as well take them off, now that you know.

(Dorothy and the others remove their spectacles. Dorothy slips hers into the pocket of her apron; Scarecrow puts his in his coat pocket; Woodman lays his out of the way on the cabinet. Lion lays his on the bench. Oz continues his story. Leaning over to Dorothy).

By the way, I was terribly afraid of those Wicked Witches, and so pleased when your house fell on one of them. Though now that you've melted the other, I'm ashamed to say I can't keep my promises.

DOROTHY *(emphatically)*. I think you're a very bad man.

OZ. Oh, no, my dear. I'm really a very good man—but a very bad Wizard.

SCARECROW *(rising)*. Can't you give me brains?

OZ. You don't need them. You're learning something every day.

SCARECROW. Maybe so. But I won't be happy till you give me some brains.

(Oz looks at him carefully, then sighs).

OZ *(rising)*. Very well. I'll stuff your head with brains.

SCARECROW *(whooping with joy)*. Oh, thank you, thank you!

OZ *(Raising a warning finger)*. But mind! I can't tell you how to use them. You must find that out for yourself.

SCARECROW *(beside himself)*. Oh, I'll find a way, never fear!

OZ *(to Dorothy)*. Dorothy, you'll have to help me.

(He goes to the throne and Dorothy stands waiting for instructions. Oz beckons to her) The throne must be placed—so.

(Together, they turn the throne so that anyone sitting in it is facing directly front. Beckoning to Scarecrow) Sit here on the throne, please.

SCARECROW *(drawing back, overawed)*. Me! On the throne?

OZ *(crossing to Scarecrow)*. Why not, my friend? When I've finished with you, you'll have more brains to rule with than ever I had.

(Oz waves Scarecrow toward the throne, and he goes and sits, sniggering self-consciously. Oz crosses up to the cabinet, taking from it an oversized cereal box, marked "BRAN" in large letters, and a sewing basket, containing scissors, needle and thread, and a paper of pins. Meanwhile, Scarecrow is carrying on a conversation with Dorothy, who is standing beside him).

SCARECROW *(singing)*. Tol-de-ri-de-oh! I'm going to get my brains at last-de-oh! Then won't you be proud of me, Dorothy!

DOROTHY *(simply)*. I've always liked you the way you are.

SCARECROW. That's nice of you, but wait till you hear the splendid thoughts my new brains will turn out.

(Oz crosses back to the throne with the box of bran and the sewing basket. He gives them to Dorothy to hold, first removing the cover of the sewing basket and slipping it over the bottom of the basket. He lifts out the scissors).

OZ *(standing behind Scarecrow).* Remove your hat, please.

(Scarecrow does so, holding it on his lap. Oz snips the scissors down the back of Scarecrow's head).

You'll have to excuse me for making a hole in your head, but that's the only way I can fill it with brains.

SCARECROW *(genially).* Oh, that's all right. You can take my head off, if you like—just as long as it's a better one when you put it on again.

OZ. That won't be necessary.

(Oz removes some straw, presumably from Scarecrow's head, but actually from under the collar of his coat. Then Oz reaches into the sewing basket for the paper of pins and unrolls it).

(winking at Dorothy) These will make him sharp!

(Tittering at his own pun, he rolls up the paper of pins and stuffs it in Scarecrow's head, under top of coat).

SCARECROW *(yelping).* Ooooooo! Ouch! What you got there? A beehive? Ow!

(Now Oz takes the box of bran from Dorothy and holds it high for Scarecrow to see).

OZ. This is a bran-new idea!

(He titters again, and shakes the box vigorously behind Scarecrow's head. Scarecrow wriggles and squeals).

SCARECROW. Hey! You tickle!

(He gets hiccoughs from giggling. Oz returns bran-box to Dorothy, and takes a threaded needle from the basket. He pretends to sew up the hole in Scarecrow's head).

OZ. A stitch here—a loop there—and there—and here—and this way—and that way—and—

(he reaches into the basket for the scissors)—we're all done!

(He snips the thread) There!

(Oz steps back to admire his handiwork) You're a great man, now—with lots of bran-new brains.

(Scarecrow feels all over his head, pleased and proud).

DOROTHY *(curiously).* How do you feel?

(Scarecrow pricks his finger on the top of his head. He jumps).

SCARECROW. Sharp!

(He sucks his finger) Of course, when I get used to my brains, I shall know everything.

63

WOODMAN *(rising and crossing to C)*. How about my heart?

(Oz returns the scissors, needle and thread to the basket, takes it and the bran-box from Dorothy, and crosses to Woodman).

OZ. I think you're wrong to want a heart. If you only knew it, you're lucky not to have one.

WOODMAN *(loftily)*. That's a matter of opinion.

OZ. Well—in that case, I have just the heart for you.

(He crosses up to the cabinet and puts the sewing basket and bran-box inside. Then he takes out a red heart with a loop at the top for the purpose of hanging).

It's not a sad heart, and it's not a timid heart.

(He holds it up, coming DC. to Woodman) Isn't it a beauty?

WOODMAN *(goggle-eyed)*. Oh, yes! But is it a kind heart?

OZ *(hanging the heart on the Woodman's breast)*. Very kind. There! Now you have a heart any man might be proud of.

WOODMAN *(fondling the heart)*. Thank you.

OZ *(waving aside Woodman's gratitude)*. Don't mention it.

(Woodman crosses to Dorothy and Scarecrow in high spirits, and shows them his heart. Lion has risen, and plucks the sleeves of Oz's coat. Oz springs back, startled).

Oh!

LION *(anxiously)*. Remember me? You promised to give me courage.

OZ. Did I?

(Recollecting) Oh, of course! But you have plenty of courage, I'm sure.

LION *(moaning)*. No, I haven't. I'm just about the cowardliest Lion that ever roared.

OZ. All you need is confidence in yourself. Everyone's afraid when he faces danger. True courage is in facing it when you are afraid, and you've done that dozens of times.

LION. Yes, but I'm scared just the same. Please give me the sort of courage that'll make me forget I'm afraid.

OZ. All right. I'll get it for you.

(Oz crosses to the throne and disappears off UL. around the backing. Scarecrow tiptoes upstage and peeps around the backing, off UL., making excited gestures and muffled exclamations of pleasure to Lion at what he sees. Suddenly Scarecrow scurries back to the

group, and Oz re-enters, carrying a green dipper. He goes straight to Lion with it).

Drink this.

LION *(backing away a little).* What is it?

OZ. Well, when it's inside you, it will be courage. You know courage is always inside one.

(Lion takes the dipper from Oz, and laps till the dipper is empty. He heaves a great sigh and licks his chops, finally wiping his mouth with his tail).

How do you feel now?

LION *(roaring).* Full of courage!

(He strides over to the others, and starts sparring with Scarecrow and Woodman. Dorothy crosses to Oz).

DOROTHY *(shaking her finger at Oz).* You Great and Terrible— Humbug!

OZ *(sheepishly).* How can I help being a humbug, when people make me do things that everybody knows can't be done?

(He indicates the others, who are now admiring their "gifts" from Oz, near the throne).

Look at them. They already had what they wanted, if only they'd known it.

(The others turn excitedly to Dorothy and hurry over to her, Scarecrow leading).

SCARECROW. Dorothy, we're so happy, we'll bust if we don't do something! Will you dance a little prance with us?

(He leaps into the air, trying to click his heels together, but tumbles to the floor).

DOROTHY *(laughing).* You mean, chance a little prance, don't you?

SCARECROW *(sniggering self-consciously as the Woodman and Lion pick him up).* Yes, I suppose I do. But will you?

DOROTHY. Of course, I will!

(She crosses to Scarecrow, curtsies, and starts singing "Chance a Prance"; the words are set to the tune of "Soldier, Soldier, Will You Marry Me?" Oz goes to the bench and sits. Woodman and Lion move over to the throne, out of the way).

Scarecrow, Scarecrow, will you dance with me,
In your coat of straw and hay?

(Scarecrow executes a few eccentric steps around Dorothy to her R., his legs buckling under him from time to time. Dorothy catches him whenever he is about to fall).

SCARECROW. I'll chance a prance, a merry little dance,
In my golden straw array.

(Dorothy goes over to Lion and curtsies).

DOROTHY. Courageous Lion, will you dance with us,

SCARECROW. A straw man—

DOROTHY. —and a maid?

(Lion bows with great dignity, and gives his L. arm to Dorothy. Together they stroll over to Scarecrow, pass in front of him, and Lion takes his place on Scarecrow's right).

LION. I'll chawnce a prawnce, a merry little dawnce,
Of fun I nevah was afraid.

(Dorothy goes over to Woodman and curtsies).

DOROTHY. Woodman, Woodman, will you dance with us,
In your coat of polished tin?

(Woodman and Dorothy polka-step R., pass in front of Scarecrow and Lion, and Woodman takes his place R. of them).

WOODMAN. I'll chance a prance, a merry little dance,
For I always enjoy a spin.

(Woodman and Dorothy spin around. Dorothy goes DL. to Toto. She snaps her fingers, and he sits up "begging").

DOROTHY. Toto, Toto, will you dance with us,
Though you're just a Kansas pup?

(Toto stands on his hind legs and frisks around Dorothy as they cross R. He barks in rhythm to the tune what might be the following stanza).

TOTO. I'll chance a prance, a merry little dance,
For I need a shaking up.

(Toto shakes himself into position R. of Woodman. Dorothy takes her place in the center of the line-up, between Lion and Woodman. Now all her partners face Dorothy and go down on one knee, left hand over heart, right arms extended).

PARTNERS. Dorothy dear, will you dance with us,
In your dress of white and blue?

(Dorothy curtsies L. and R).

DOROTHY. Why, can't you see how proud I'd be
To dance with gentlemen like you?

(They all "la-la" the tune through once, and Dorothy waltzes with each one in turn, in this order: Scarecrow, Lion, Woodman, Toto. As she finishes her turn with Toto, Dorothy notices Oz sit-

ting forlornly on the bench by himself. She goes to him and curt-sies).

Mr. Wizard, will you dance with me?

OZ *(spoken).* What for?

DOROTHY *(pulling Oz to his feet).* Oh, just because!

(Oz waltzes with Dorothy grotesquely).

OZ. I'll chance a prance, a merry little dance,
Because I'm the Humbug of Oz.

(He breaks away from Dorothy and speaks earnestly).

Oh, how can I get you back to Kansas!

DOROTHY *(fervently).* If only you can, I'll forgive you everything!

OZ *(tapping his forehead).* I'll have to think about it—hard—for two or three days.

(He bows abruptly to Dorothy) Excuse me, while I think.

(And without another word, or a backward glance, he turns on his heel, marches up the steps, and off).

DOROTHY *(gaping).* Well!

(The others are struck dumb at the sudden exit of Oz. When they are able to speak and move again, which is almost instantly, they crowd around Dorothy, all talking at once. After a few excited barks, Toto goes DL. and curls up by the proscenium for a snooze).

ALL. What happened! . . . Is he angry? . . . Why did he leave like that? . . . Did he say where he was going?

DOROTHY *(stuffing her fingers in her ears).* Oh, shush!

(The hubbub subsides).

He's gone off to think.

SCARECROW. To think! That's my job, now.

DOROTHY. Then please think of a way to get me back to Kansas.

(Scarecrow goes to the bench, sits, and assumes a "thinking" pose. The others watch instantly. After a moment, Scarecrow chuckles to himself).

(curiously) What's the matter?

SCARECROW *(hugging himself and pointing to his forehead).* Wonderful thoughts! Wonderful!

DOROTHY. Tell us!

67

SCARECROW (*shaking his head*). Can't. You wouldn't understand them.

(*Dorothy sighs with disappointment, and waits for further developments. Suddenly she exclaims and runs to Scarecrow, pressing her hands against his head*).

DOROTHY (*warningly*). Oh, do be careful! Your head is bulging with thoughts, and the pins are sticking out all over!

(*In a panic*) Oh, oh! Stop thinking! It's going to burst!

(*Woodman raises his axe to ward off what seems will be the explosion of Scarecrow's brains. Lion scampers to the throne for shelter, crouching behind it. Both Dorothy and Scarecrow press mightily against his head, and the crisis passes. Everybody relaxes*).

SCARECROW (*sinking back on the bench, exhausted*). Whew! That was a narrow escape.

(*To Dorothy, excitedly*) But I've thought of a way to get you back to Kansas!

DOROTHY (*eagerly*). How?

(*Lion comes out from behind the throne. Woodman lowers his axe*).

SCARECROW. Call the Winged Monkeys, and they'll carry you there!

DOROTHY (*overjoyed*). I never thought of that!

(*She reaches up to the Golden Cap on her head, as Lion comes forward to C.*).

LION. That won't work. The Winged Monkeys belong to this country and can't leave it.

DOROTHY. How do you know?

LION. The Monkey King told me so.

(*Dorothy is ready to cry with disappointment. Woodman crosses to her and puts his arm around her comfortingly*).

WOODMAN. That's too bad.

(*Scarecrow again assumes his "thinking" pose. At this moment, the Soldier with Green Whiskers enters UR. all of a fluster. He stops halfway down the steps and salutes*).

SOLDIER. Attention, please! The most marvelous thing has happened! Oz has gone to visit his brother!

DOROTHY. His brother!

WOODMAN. What's so marvelous about that?

68

(Soldier looks down his nose disdainfully at Woodman, and points up).

SOLDIER. His brother lives in the clouds.

DOROTHY *(moving to the foot of the steps).* In the clouds!

SOLDIER. That's what he said.

DOROTHY *(plaintively).* You mean, Oz has left us?

SOLDIER. Yes.

(Sniffing) Isn't it sad?

(Breaking down) He sailed away in a balloon to visit his brother in the clouds. He gave me this letter for you.

(Soldier hands letter to Dorothy, and then sits on the steps, sobbing quietly. Dorothy opens the letter).

DOROTHY *(reading).* "Dear Dorothy. I'm tired of being a humbug. I'd rather be a balloonist in a circus. I've appointed the Wise Scarecrow to rule over the Emerald City in my place. The people will be proud of him, because there's not another city in the world that is ruled by a stuffed man. Au revoir. OZ. P. S. I'm sorry about Kansas."

(There is a moment of stunned silence, then Dorothy breaks into a wail) Now what are we going to do?

(Scarecrow rises snappily and swaggers to the throne).

SCARECROW. Do? Do? Why, do as we please?

(He stands before the throne, musing) Hmmmm. From a pole in a farmer's cornfield to King of the Emerald City. Not bad, not bad!

(He sits on the throne, first turning it around to its original position).

WOODMAN. I should like to cry a little because Oz is gone. After all, he gave me my lovely heart.

(To Dorothy) Will you please wipe away my tears, so I won't rust?

DOROTHY *(sympathetically).* Of course.

(Woodman weeps, and Dorothy carefully wipes away his tears with her handkerchief, one by one, as they fall. Lion sniffs and wipes his nose with his tail).

LION *(querolously).* He made me as brave as any beast that ever lived. If only he'd taken a dose of the same courage he gave me, he'd have been brave, too.

WOODMAN *(to Dorothy, as she wipes away his last tear).* Thank you.

(He goes up to the cabinet, gets his oil can from Dorothy's basket, and oils his jaws thoroughly, to guard against mishap).

SCARECROW *(from his eminence on the throne).* If Dorothy would only be contented to live here, we might all be happy together.

DOROTHY *(crossing to the throne).* But I don't want to live here. I want to live in Kansas, with Aunt Em.

WOODMAN *(turning from the cabinet).* Well, but where is Kansas?

SCARECROW. Let's ask the Soldier.

(Raising his voice regally) You! Soldier with Green Whiskers!

(Soldier starts up from the steps, where he has been sitting, mourning the departure of Oz. He salutes in confusion. Scarecrow grandly beckons him to the throne, and Soldier advances timidly).

SCARECROW *(indicating Dorothy).* This little girl wants to go home to Kansas. Do you know the way?

SOLDIER *(gloomily).* I haven't the faintest notion which way it is.

(Encouragingly) But the first thing to do is cross the desert, and then it ought to be easy to find Kansas.

DOROTHY. How can I cross the desert?

SOLDIER *(shrugging).* I don't know. Nobody ever has.

DOROTHY *(earnestly).* Isn't there any one who can help me?

SOLDIER *(thoughtfully).* Glinda might.

SCARECROW. Who is Glinda?

(Woodman and Lion move in, listening attentively).

SOLDIER. The Good Witch of the South. Her castle stands on the edge of the desert, and she may know a way to cross it.

DOROTHY. Is her castle far from here?

SOLDIER. About a three-days' journey. Go straight South, to the Quadling Country.

(Warningly) But watch out for the Fighting Trees.

DOROTHY. Fighting Trees? Do you mean trees that fight?

SOLDIER. I do. Their branches bend down and seize you, and toss you right back where you came from.

SCARECROW *(rising in protest).* But where we came from would be right here where we are!

DOROTHY. Oh, dear! That wouldn't be any good.

(She sinks down on the throne steps and begins to cry).

70

It's no use! I'll never, never, never get back to Kansas!

(She sobs in complete despair. Her friends gather around and try to comfort her).

SCARECROW. There, there! Of course you will!

LION. Don't you worry, Dorothy. No fighting trees are going to stop us! I'll fix 'em!

(He doubles up his paws into fists).

WOODMAN *(trying to cheer up Dorothy with a bit of nonsense).* You musn't cry so! You'll rust your joints!

(Music: faint and far-away. Soldier catches the sound of it and bends his head to listen).

SOLDIER *(holding up his hand for silence).* Shhhhh! Be quiet!

(Dorothy stops crying) I hear something.

SCARECROW. What?

SOLDIER. I don't know.

(He moves toward the steps UR.) But something is going—to—happen!

(And something does happen. A large bright red balloon floats down from above into their midst. There is a letter attached to the string. Dorothy and Scarecrow run over to pick up the balloon. Toto wakes up from his nap).

DOROTHY. It's a balloon! And there's a letter tied to it.

SCARECROW *(examining the inscription on the envelope).* It's addressed to you, Dorothy.

DOROTHY. So it is!

(With a gasp of surprise) Why, that's Oz's handwriting!

(She opens the envelope and takes out of piece of notepaper. The others crowd around).

(reading) "Dear Dorothy. As I was passing over the Quadling Country, I dropped a note to Glinda the Good, asking her to have tea with you next Friday afternoon. The Quadling Country is right next door to the China Country, so naturally Glinda prefers China tea. Love. OZ. P. S. She may be able to get you back to Kansas."

(Dorothy clasps the letter to her bosom) Oh, do you think she can?

SOLDIER. If anyone can, Glinda can.

71

DOROTHY (*impatiently*). But Friday's three whole days away. I can't wait that long!

(*Fanfare is heard off UR.*).

SOLDIER. You won't have to wait that long. Here's Glinda now!

(*Fanfare is repeated. Glinda The Good is revealed standing in the doorway UR., smiling at them. She is young and beautiful. Her hair falls in flowing ringlets over her shoulders. Her dress is pure white*).

GLINDA (*coming down the steps to Dorothy*). Are you Dorothy?

DOROTHY (*curtsying*). Yes, ma'am.

GLINDA (*looking at her kindly*). What can I do for you, my child?

(*Soldier goes up the steps and stands on guard beside the doorway. Dorothy speaks rapidly, as if she fears she will be interrupted before she has finished*).

DOROTHY. The cyclone blew me to the Land of Oz, and I want to get back to Kansas, because Aunt Em will surely think something dreadful has happened to me and that will make her put on mourning, and unless the crops are better this year than they were last, I'm sure Uncle Henry can't afford it.

(*Glinda laughs and bends over, kissing Dorothy's cheek*).

GLINDA. Bless your dear heart! We'll find a way to get you home. But first, give me your Golden Cap.

(*Dorothy takes it off, and gives it to Glinda*) Now I can ask three favors of the Winged Monkeys.

(*She turns to the Woodman*) Tin Woodman, what will become of you when Dorothy leaves this country?

WOODMAN. The Winkies were very kind to me, and wanted me to rule over them after the Wicked Witch died.

GLINDA. I shall command the Winged Monkeys—

(*she holds out the Golden Cap at arm's length in front of her*)

—to carry you to the Land of the Winkies. Your brains may not be as large to look at as the Scarecrow's but you're really brighter than he is—

(*appropriate reactions from Woodman and Scarecrow*) —when you're well polished—

(*reverse reactions*) —and I'm sure you'll rule the Winkies wisely and well.

WOODMAN (*enthusiastically*). I should like nothing better than to rule over them forever!

(*Glinda smiles at him and passes on to Lion*).

72

GLINDA *(patting his head).* And you, Courageous Lion, what will you do?

LION. In the Land of the Munchkins, lies a grand old forest, and if I could only get back to it, I'd pass my life very happily there as King of the Beasts.

GLINDA. And so you shall. My second command to the Winged Monkeys will be to carry you to your forest.

(She crosses to Scarecrow) And now, Wise Scarecrow, what will you do when Dorothy has left us?

SCARECROW. I shall stay here in the Emerald City.

(Proudly) Oz has made me its ruler! But I would like to visit the Woodman and Lion once in a while. The only thing that worries me is how to get through the Forest of Fighting Trees.

GLINDA. That's easy. My third command to the Winged Monkeys will be that they carry you safely over the Forest of Fighting Trees. It would be a shame to deprive the people of so ~~a ruler.~~

SCARECROW *(simpering).* Am I really wonderful?

GLINDA. You are—unusual.

DOROTHY *(to Glinda).* You're so good. But you have~~i~~ yet how I'll get back to Kansas.

GLINDA *(smiling).* Your silver slippers will carry you

DOROTHY *(looking down at her feet).* My silver slippe~~r~~

GLINDA. Didn't you know that they have a magic cha~~r~~

DOROTHY. Yes, but I didn't know what it was.

GLINDA. They will take you anywhere.

DOROTHY *(incredulously).* Do you mean I could have gone back to Aunt Em the very first day I came to this country?

GLINDA *(nodding).* Yes, my dear.

SCARECROW *(to Dorothy).* But then I wouldn't have had my wonderful brains.

WOODMAN. Nor I, my lovely heart.

LION. And I should have lived a coward forever.

DOROTHY. That's true—and I'm glad I was able to help all of you. But now I think I should like to go home.

GLINDA. Just knock the heels of your slippers together three times, and say where you want to go.

(Lights: slow dim. Music).

(The moment to say goodbye has come. Dorothy looks from one to the other of her three good friends, and a lump comes into her throat. Lion moves impulsively to her, and she throws her arms around his neck, patting his big head tenderly).

DOROTHY.   Goodbye, dear Lion.

(Woodman begins to weep in a way most dangerous to his joints. Dorothy gets out her handkerchief and wipes his eyes, then her own).

(through her tears) You musn't cry.   You'll rust your joints.

(Woodman gets control of his emotion, and Dorothy goes to Scarecrow. She hugs him tight, sobbing in his arms, pressing her face against his soft, stuffed body).

SCARECROW *(smoothing her hair).* Now, now, Dorothy. You musn't greet Aunt Em with hiccoughs and a shiny nose.

DOROTHY *(wiping her nose).* N-n-no.

GLINDA *(urging gently).* Better get started, dear, before the sun sets.

(Dorothy turns to Toto and whistles).

DOROTHY.   Come, Toto! We're going home.

(Toto barks and bounds over to Dorothy. She takes him solemnly by the collar, steps forward, draws in a deep breath, and claps her heels together three times).

(joyfully) Take me home to Aunt Em!

(Everyone, except Dorothy and Toto, freeze in a tableau. Music: crescendo. Dorothy and Toto move down to the apron of the stage, as if in a dream. Toto sits, looking at Dorothy. She stands expectant, looking out front. Lights: dim on tableau).

House Curtain closes behind Dorothy and Toto.

Front lights up full. Music: down under.

Dorothy gazes about her in wonder. From the back of the auditorium, Right Stage, comes Aunt Em's voice, calling from far off, sounding like a bell ringing over the miles).

AUNT EM.   Dor-o-theeeee . . . Dor-o-thee . . .

(Dorothy turns slowly in the direction of the voice, and a smile of recognition lights up her face. Toto pricks up his ears and listens, too).

DOROTHY *(hardly breathing).* Toto! It's Aunt Em! We're in Kansas! We're home!

(Now Aunt Em's voice sounds near at hand, natural, and full of love).

74

AUNT EM. Dorothy! My darling child! Where in the world have you been?

(Dorothy starts for the Right Stage steps, with Toto at her heels).

DOROTHY. In the Land of Oz!

(She runs down the aisle, with Toto behind her, barking excitedly).

But, oh, Aunt Em! I'm so glad to be home again!

(Music: up).

END OF ACT THREE

CURTAIN